Songs of Stars

Songs of Stars

Edited by
Harish K Thakur

ANAMIKA PUBLISHERS & DISTRIBUTORS (P) LTD.
4697/3, 21A, Ansari Road, Daryaganj, New Delhi 110 002
Phones: 011-2328 1655, 011-43708938
E-mail: anamikapublishers@yahoo.co.in

First Published 2021

ISBN 978-81-750900-0-8

PRINTED IN INDIA

Published by Anamika Publishers & Distributors (P) Ltd., 4697/3, 21A, Ansari Road, Daryaganj, New Delhi 110002. Typeset by Shivani Computers, Delhi 110093 and Printed at Vikas Computer & Printers, Tronica City, Ghaziabad

अनंतं वासुकि शेष पद्मनाभं चे कम्बलम् ।
शङ्खपाल धार्तराष्ट्र तक्षकं कालियं तथा ॥
एतानि नव नामानि नागानां च महात्मनाम् ।
सायंकाले पठेन्नित्यं प्रातः काले विशेषतः ॥
तस्मे विषभयं नास्ति सर्वत्र विजयीं भवेत् ।

Contents

Preface and Acknowledgements

Today humanity is divided over the astral influences on life and events on earth and elsewhere, if any, but the occult sciences do have significance in human lives denying which may be as fatal as the high tides during the lunar phases. Astrology primarily relies on the belief that human life and happenings in the world do have a strong bearing of the effects of the complex web of star cast (planets which are near in distance and the constellations of stars which form a collective force) spread overhead during the time of a happening or birth of a human. It has been observed with thousands of instances that birth at a particular time when the star positions are negative or debilitated the chance of survival is less and this requires to be cured at the earliest if possible.

Although through the 'Cartesian or Rationalist view' of science or the 'hypothetico-deductive view' as followed by Socrates and the comparisons by Aristotle the course of astrology has been made difficult and the substance of astrology challenged, yet I believe that 'absence of evidence is not the evidence of absence' and since humans have failed to answer hundreds of questions of metaphysics where science too feels deceived by reason the case for astrological predictions remains strong.

Several years back about 18 Nobel Laureates and 172 other leading scientists of the world raised their voice against the science that astrology claimed to be. In the ensuing years many scientists like Shawn Carlson and Barth and Bennett proved astrology only to be a chance explanation but the existence of mysteriously precise predictions since earliest times keep the debate live no matter astrology is reduced to a pseudo-science.

It was with this belief that in 2009, I started writing about stars, *nakshtras, bhavas, yogas* etc. The literary devices of free verse and irregular meter have been followed to make the presentation more interesting and musical. The planets and *nakshtras,* their properties that they transmit to the characters under their influence, have been explicated in poetry. The exigency of poetry form sometimes makes the presentation vague and imprecise but that has to be scuttled as part of art by readers and the author apologizes for that. For making the volume more interesting a chapter on zodiac signs by Prof. Som P Ranchan has also been inducted. The chapter includes zodiac signs, their descriptions, practical realization and a personal correspondence. Namita Sethi adds a significant section on crystals and stones and their curative qualities to the book. The views expressed by authors are their own and should be taken as individual standings. Therefore, the current endeavour is presented to the readers in the shape of a slim volume with the hope that it would be welcomed and cherished with all its pros and cons. Anamika Publishers deserves special thanks, since astrology is a rare take today.

The work is divisible into six chapters. Chapter one is on *Songs of Stars*; chapter two *Nakshtras (Constellations): Properties and Predictions*; chapter three *Planetary Properties*; chapter four *Introduction to Zodiac* by Prof. Som P. Ranchan; chapter five *The Twelve Houses or Bhavas* and chapter six *The*

Major Yogas. Chapter seven by Prof. Namita Sethi discusses various stones and crystals. I express my gratitude to her for editing and proof reading services. I extend special thanks to Prof. Mahidhar Sharma, Prof. Parveen Bhatia and Pandit Jai Prakash Sharma from whom I have benefitted a lot over the decades. The slim volume is an offering in the genre of a general reader's handbook with the hope that it would be received widely and taken critically.

Harish K Thakur

Chapter-1

Songs of Stars

Harish K Thakur

Sun

Sun, the almighty
Represents the Lagna
The personality
The fire inside, the vanity

It epitomizes the soul
The fire, crimson, copper
And the body whole
Bone, eye, stomach and heart
The ambers of its morale
Sweep the hurdles
The valor of enemy apart

Sun is father, state, the reign
In exaltation goes berserk
In triangle or house number ten
And no one can restrain it
From the throw of prowess

That flows from its arms
When the enemy it aggresses

It is warrior, robust, strong
Fighter, sportive, sinful
Audacious to rule
It commits the blunders prime
If shadowed by Rahu or Saturn
Then leads to collusion or crime

It is resplendent and bright,
Spews and splatters the light
A man with Sun strong
Shall have to glory a right

And lo! if the Sun is malefic
Would be tyrannous and terrific
On self and the other

It's scrawny fire kills the hunger
Weakens heart, lessens sight
Valor and name undergoes shrill
And fracture the bones
With all its skill

So Ruby would save your light
And galvanize the plight
Broken and shattered by rotten Sun
Restore the crimson in your life

Moon

Though small in size
But its short distance from earth
Maximizes
The impact of moon
Over the life
Of man and creatures
And the strife

Moon is water
Moon is wave
Moon is emotion
It makes the heart kind
Greater the feelings
For mother devotion
Would be there
When moon is king

And when the moon
Is on the rise and high flight
Up goes the passion
The marvel, the feet, the earth, the morale
And the maternal compassion
Would flow to you
Like the flow of the light

It is mind, it is wisdom
The blessings of the king
The mother, land would come
In your way
From the Moon's wallet

If not in cash
The letters great
Glaring, creative, original, gold
And not the trash

When moon is on the slide
From full to low
Slumps the heart
The tides and glow
And weaker the crescent
Weaker the mind, mother's health
Flow of blood not-magnificent
If shadowed by Rahu
Or malefic Saturn
One can go amuck
Or for self kill
Startling can be the turn
In one's life

Jaundice, blood pressure, gynae infections
Insanity, odima and the hallucinations
Are the fizzles
And the periods unstable

Mercury

Blinking eye often shy
Under the thrash of burning sun
Instantly here, instantly there
No one knows
Its wilder turn

Mercury is a child
Who runs wild
If unreined by the planets hot
Softer, swifter temper it gives
caressing makes it
Thoroughly mild

It makes one flicker
Like staggering mercury
As if a walk on fire or ice
Swifter than lightening
Sharper than neurons
Faster than wind
It scampers nice

Faster the mind
Sweeter the tongue
In commerce, accounts
Or editing benign
Mercury, if enjoys sound hold
Can make you teller
Orator, doctor, writer
Middleman and foreteller
All in its single fold

In relation Mercury is sister
Daughter and father's sister
Exalted shall take you
To writing or journalism
Mathematics and if duly
Conjoined by Saturn to barrister
And debilitated mercury

Can hassle the tongue
Cause lukederma
And skin burn
If joined by stronger sun
It weakens the neurons
Pinches the skin
And smacks digestion

Its colour is green
So wear emerald
If mercury is lean
And worship Maa Durga
Lord Vishnu and Ganesha
Eat green vegetables and beans

Jupiter

Sun, Mars, Saturn, Venus
Among the planets all
Mind, wisdom, spirit and truth
Of Jupiter stands tall

It is colossal, mature, sturdy
Planner, guide, educator
Cool, visionary, philosopher
Seer, ascetic, and mentor

Guru the man will be
And lord of followers many
Sparkle like a sun
In the dark deeps uncanny

Teachers, statesmen, scholars
Administrators, managers all
Owe to a strong Jupiter
From whom, the state's blessings fall

Blest are those lighted by Jupiter
For it is the planet of 'greater fortunes'
Knowledge, wisdom, piety
Vision, intuition all it tunes

It sees the world
With the eye fulgent
Colossus it is among the stars
And constellations
And reads the palms veiled
Turns one benevolent

Debilitated Jupiter
Brings the woes many
Like jaundice, cholesterol, thoughtlessness
Obesity, stomach ache and carelessness

Venus

The queen of beauty
The queen of love
Besides courtship, marriage, sex
Venus stands far above

It is bright, illumined
As if damsel in heaven
Fire of eye

Ray of mind
Tippler's tip in tavern

All creation belongs to it
Since Venus represents feminine earth
And Mar's marvel, Jupiter's wisdom
Sun's wrath loose the worth
Until semen and fertility
Venus does put-forth

Art, music, fiction, drama
Men and women of Venus should try
Since it triggers all creation
And higher one must fly

Venus brings wealth
And all the luxuries of life
And takes the man away
From poverty, struggle and strife

Weakened Venus leads to hardships
Dullness in life and genital diseases
Bronchial ailments, choked lungs
Diabetes, urine and cough problems

Mars

Young, youthful, strong, passionate
Crimson, hot and royal is Mars
Lightening in tresses, fire in barrel
Swelling biceps, always at war

Mars is brother, sister and friend
Lover, soldier, enemy strong
In the lanes of Venus and Urvashi
Uninvited does it throng

Imposing shall he be
In every sphere of life
And emulating in disposition
In sport, struggle and strife

If joined by Venus
Makes one lascivious
By Saturn conspirer, plotter
By Jupiter a high rank officer
And if by Rahu and tail extorter

Power is the mantra
And karma the tantra,
Fate in the hands makes sense
Nothing afar with Mar's incandescence

Poorly placed Mars
Shall make one audacious
Quarrelsome, short tempered
Marshal, scoundrel, malicious

In debilitation causes anemia, accidents
Boils, muscular dystrophy, blood pressure
And the body flavescent

Saturn

Among the planets all
When scary destiny falls
Saturn is the planet remote
Justice, truth, penalty
Failure, feud, grief
All that the blue planet denotes

Saturn is skeleton weak and old
Lazarus, lame, king of darkness
Oblique in aspect, unforgiving
Gives mass following great
Judge and the law ultimate

In dark robe shall he march
From brightness, sun and moon
With all worldly passion
Against the wisdom of Jupiter
Divinity of Uranus,
Not in expansion but in recession
To the abyss infinite

Against the smaller disasters of Mars
It leads to greater loss
Of mind, health and wealth
Man, community and public gloss

Strong Saturn bestows long life
Wealth, name, and triumph over snags
And greater share in public life

Engineers, builders, contractors
Property dealers, brokers and surgeons
All have an element of Saturn
Without which their fate
Can never take due turn

Saturn in lagna if poorly placed
Gives suspicion, over cautiousness
Sluggishness, non-action and
Makes nervous system frail
Brings misfortunes in the longer trail

Friend for Venus, enemy to Sun
All that flows from Saturn's strand
Shall never return
Until the blue eyed sapphire shine
In the native's hand

Uranus

Uranus is the planet next
That rules the wit and mind the best
Unlike the orthodox Saturn
And the wisdom wide of Jupiter
It governs the creative impulse
The lightening flash sublime
And bestows the intelligence divine

It confers the best to one
The original, the real, the novel
The rational, thinking, intellect
Intuition, and the knack of forecast

Wow! all in one

Electrical engineering, computers
Electronics, IT, shares, forecasting
Are the pursuits it proffers
And when it comes to eclipse one
In a flash does it rob

Instant ups, instant downs,
In life, business, fate
Like mercury does it crown
And when it comes to instant end
In a lightening does it descend

Uranus governs the number
Of lesser fortunes
That is the number four
And through cardiac arrest, accidents
Tragic shocks bring one to floor

Neptune

The lunar octave is Neptune
That rules the number of greater fortune
The number seven
And picks the bubbles from eyes
To form its own heaven

Generational impact it has
Over the people for long
Since it stays in a sign for years thirteen
Its upshots there prolong

Insight for occult he shall have
And a frenzy for orange and saffron
Lulled by the waves divine
Shall he wander and estrange

Ascetic, eccentric, divine soul
Not the fragments small
But cosmos whole
A river in the eye
And higher shall fly
The dreams, thoughts of the native

Prone to hallucinations and superstitions
He shall have sharper intuition
Strong the dream-telling and imagery
To read the past and future
And shall have smoother sails
In the signs of water

Pluto

Pluto, the planet of energy
Revolves round the Sun for long
Higher octave of mars it is
To it the vitality of Sun belongs

Pluto forms the wider circle
And wider and wider
The number zero
From creation to destruction
The cycle it forms and
Benefactor stupendously transforms

From unsung man to hero

Like a serpent it eats its tail
And overwhelms the generation
Converges the life and strife
In its complex trail

Like the planet Mars
It is the lord of war and death
Can bring the larger annihilation
With its nuclear impulse
In times small fraction

Rahu

Darkness engulfs all
When moon descends in the South
Constricts, separates and squeezes
The positive expansion
Towards the dragons mouth

Rahu is a shadow planet
No physic does it own
Instant rise instant fall
It brings in its trail

It is a shade
A planet black
The arms of prosperity
It conveniently hacks
Until accompanied by a wiser body
Or the aspect of planet bright

That harnesses its thrust
In a positive way
And set the things upright

Like a lightening it splinters
The sun of wisdom
And sows the seeds of doubt
Fear and melancholy
Poisons the mind
Through gentle whispers
And turns the holy unholy

Epilepsy, schizophrenia
Illusion, infections
Forgetfulness, imprisonment
And depression
Are the ailments
That Rahu brings

Ketu

And then comes out another shadow
When moon descends in the south
A headless character
That thinks from the gut
Is said to have set forth

It has no sign no rulership
No friend, no head to conspire
No love for the matter worldly
No heart for wealth to aspire

It represents the other, the metaphysics
The search for the world another
No respite in the mundane
No attachment even for the mother

A man in Lagna with Ketu
Shall turn into an ascetic
A guru, a healer, a tantric
A yogi, a seeker, a shaman
For god the whole world
Shall he abandon

He can be a fine teacher
Author, predictor and reader of palms,
And can manage the Ashrams and charity
old age houses and missions
All that serves the humanity

Ketu brings division
In the houses that it affects
And causes wounds, nervous failure
Ulcers, fever and insanity
Inflammations and intestinal debility.

Its collusion with Sun or Mars
Makes it fiery, fatal
And can cause burns, accidents
And spoils the life natal

But in conjunction with Jupiter
It leads to greater heights
Saint or guru shall the native be

Spreading the knowledge and light

Ill aspected if one
shall be dud and moron
poor complexed
For equal place shall he moan
And frown at the wisdom

Cat's eye is the stone
And donation of the things white
That can ameliorate the effects
And bring the Ketu to atone

CHAPTER-2

Nakshtras : Properties and Predictions

HARISH K THAKUR

Nakshatras are the stars individual, group or constellations of many spread over the lunar mansion (the fractions or parts of ecliptic), the Sun's circular path on the celestial sphere that it appears to pursue in a year. There is controversy over the number of these fractions or parts. For many scholars they are 27 in number while for others the number is 28. These 28 fractions over the ecliptic are called Nakshtras which are personified according to the emerging shapes or patterns of stars called 'asterism' in astronomy.

The whole zodiac consists of 360 degrees and the twelve signs in number divide this entire zodiac into 13.2 degrees each. The movement of moon in each nakshtra is almost every day and in zodiac sign it stays for about 2.3 days. The twenty eight days circle of moon is causative of the brighter half (Shukla Paksha) and darker half (Krishan Paksha) of the moon or the fortnight nature of moon or lunar phases. In Indian astrology nakshtras were identified well before the zodiac signs and are primary players as compared to the latter. Even in Mahabharta there is reference to nakshtras only and to zodiac. For all the important occasions the lunar position in the nakshtra of the native is always observed. In the current chapter the primary properties of the nakshtras, their lords, planets and names in Arab Manzil (house) and Chiense Sieu (constellations) have been discussed in free verse and irregular meter. The native has been referred to as " he" which simultaneously applies to opposite sex too. The requisite curative mantras and worship has also been advised.

Nakshtras (Constellations): A View

Ashwini – I

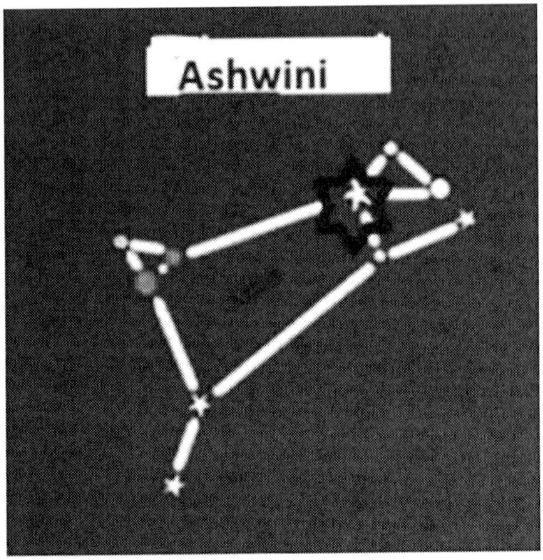

The first nakshtra in zodiacal extension
Comprising of stars two
Imagined as two horsemen
Ashwini gets the mention.
Known as 'Castor and Pollux' of the Greeks
'Leu' in the Chinese Sieu
And 'Ash -Sharatan' in the Arab Manzil

The nakshtra in Aries
Is governed by twin Ashwins or
Ashwin Kumars
Sons of Lord Sun
And by the planet Ketu.
Yet another tale goes
Calling them the healers of the Gods.
To break the monism
The creator created many forms

And the gods
Ashwin being the first.

Medium in constitution
Bright eyed, thick nosed
The native is handsome in countenance
Calm, quite, adamant in decision
Hindered life till years thirty
And shall rise after that to prominence.

Sportsman, healer, surgeon
Soldier, engineer, researcher
The native can become in life.
Shall have great married life
And a family full of sons
But due to ill-termed nature
And adamancy the hearts can't be won.
And can have issues with heart, head
Eyes and arms in prime
The native should worship Lord Ganesha
The remover of obstacles
And chant "Om Am"
And "Om Im" 108 times

Bharini – II

Bharini is second in extension
A cluster of stars forty one
Called 'Oei' in Chinese
'Arietis' in Greek and
In Arab Manzil 'Al-Bhutain'.
A triangle of stars three

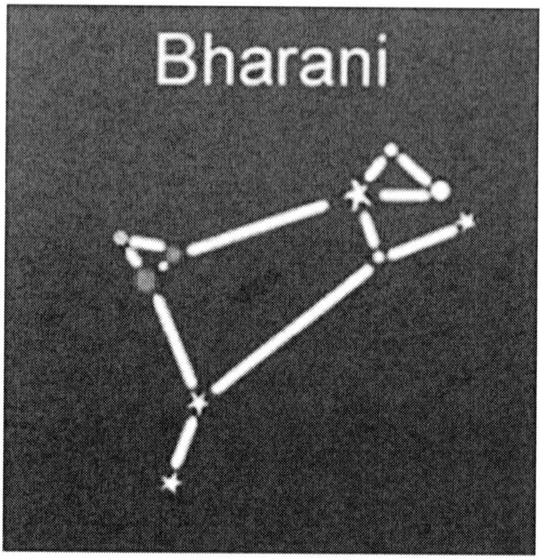

For some an elephant trunk or yoni
Or assume the vessel shape of Bharini.

Daughter of Daksha
And wife of Chandra
The Godess of luck and wealth
Bharani is governed by Yama
And the planet Venus
The death-arm of Shiva
The lord of departed spirits

Medium statured, at times tall
Large forehead, bright eyes
Pomegranate teeth
The native shall be attractive
Imposing in will, indiscreet in method
Pure and liberal at heart
To the elements of arrogance
And adamancy, a captive.

Good in education
Teacher, publisher, writer
Gynaecologist, Artist, hypnotist
Musician, hoteliers, judge, occultist
The native can be

A happy married life shall he lead
Dental problem, diabetes
Fever, apoplexy can down the native
So worshipping of Yama or Kali
And chanting of 'Om Eem' 108 times
Shall help

Kritika – III

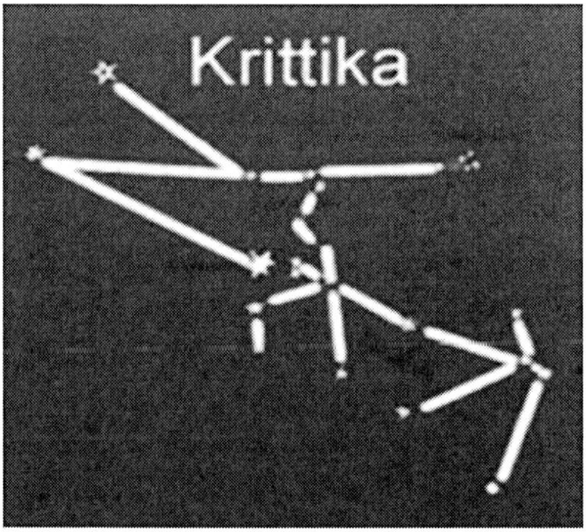

Governed by Lord Agni
And the planet Sun
The fourth in extension is' Ath Thuraiya'
'Tauri or Alcyone' of Greek or
'Mao' of Chinese Sieu

It is Kartikeya, the son of Shiva
The prime Lord
The commander of the celestial army
Of the Suras or Gods

Bereft of the goal in life
And mercurial in stance
The fire inside him shall he have
Strong will and determination
On different means in life shall he prance

He shall work at distant land
On the terms of his own'
Shall leave the friends and firms
And deceit shall he disown

Middle in height though at times tall
Emphatic and muscular in physic
At lures of different ranges in life
Shall he grow and fall

He shall have the fire
In energies shall he abound
A master fighter
Shall he grow to height
On name and fame on ground

The native should worship Sun or Kartikeya
And chant the mool mantra
"Om Im" and "Om Oo"

Rohini – IV

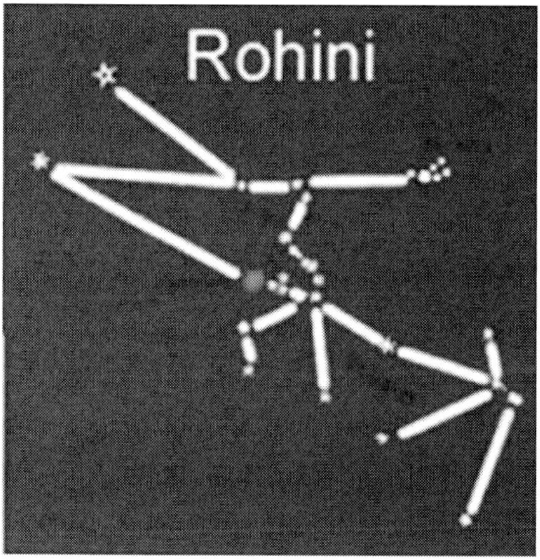

Fourth in extension in zodiac
A group of five
Lies the Nakshtra Rohini
Known as 'Alderan' in Greek
'Pi' in Chinese Sieu
And 'Ad -Dabran' in Arab Manzil
Daughter of Kashyap
Red cow or wife of moon
Is ruled by Prajapati
And the planet moon.
The frame is slim
And bright the eye
Catchy personality and developed muscles
Hearts hundreds at Rohini shall die

Short in temper
Obstinate, quarrelsome

Without aim shall one wander
Gives life to friends and loved ones
Like lightening on enemies shall thunder.

Jack of all the trades
Shall he be and weak in will,
In patience one lacks
Chemical, mechanic, milk or farm
Can be the professions in track

The river of wealth shall flow
From the maternal side
Problems in marital relation
Diseases related with blood and urine
Shall Rohinian develop
And to lower the ill effects
The native should worship cow
And chant the mool mantra
"Om Rm" and "Om Lrm" 108 times

Mrigshira – V

Fifth in extension
The three star deer
The 'Al Hakah' in Arab Manzil
'Orione' in Greek
And 'Tse' in Chinese Sieu
Stands Mrigshira
Governed by moon
Son of Tara and father of mercury

Attractive in looks

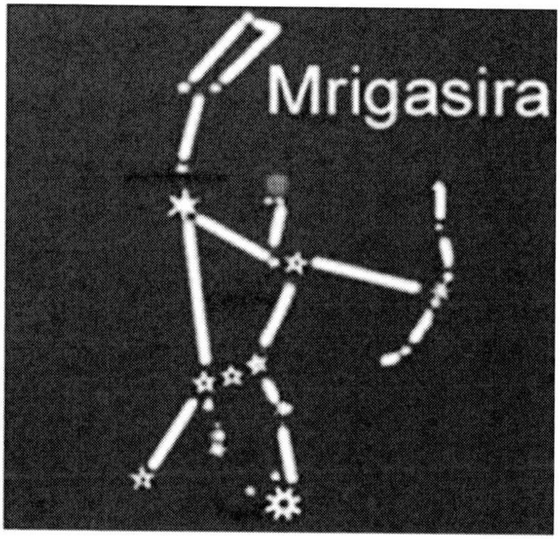

With antelope eyes
Tall in stature
Moderate in complexion and
Blind in faith
Skeptical shall be one in nature.

Till the age of thirty two
Shall lead a life of blunder
Good in education
And apt in finance
In property misfortune shall thunder

Should he not embrace death
Or illusions and perils of mind
The subject should wear a pearl
Or mantra of moon is sound
Mrigasira natives should worship Parvati
And chant the root mantra
"Om Em" 108 times

Ardra - VI

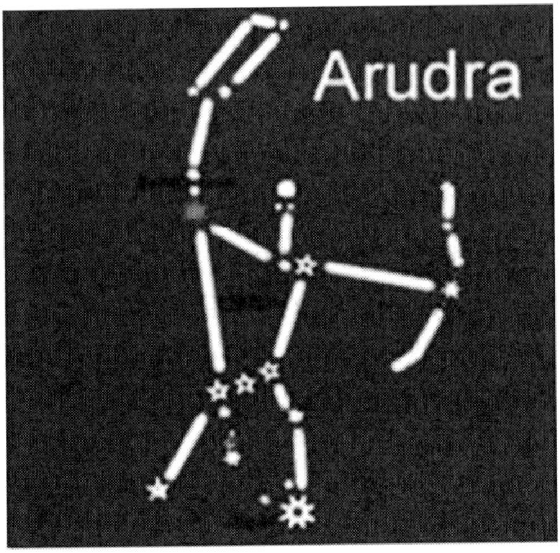

A brilliant lonestar up there
Is Ardra or "moist"
That corresponds to Ál Hanah' of Arab Manzil
Meaning a pile
'Betelgeuse' of Greeks or
'Tsan' of Chinese Sieu
For Chinese it's a constellation of many
For Arab a twin
For Hindu system it's just one
The mantle of trust
Who always doth win

Governed by 'Rudra'
And the planet Rahu
The lord of storm and destruction,
Who controls the nervous system too,
The younger brother of Indra

The incumbent shall bear
A mixture of qualities
Either fat or tall
Or slimmer in shape may he appear

He shall possess good knowledge
And will be jack of trades many
Shall fail to get the recognition
And may struggle in life to earn penny
The marriage shall be late
And if takes place early in life
Shall be forced to separate

The fortunes lay open late
From 32 to 45 years
And shall take one to the profession
Of transport, industry, fire
Or trade and communication.

Asthma, paralysis, infections
Mumps, ear pain are the troubles
The owner of the Nakshtra
The natives should worship Lord Shiva
And chant the mool mantra
"Om Aeem" 108 times

Punarvasu – VII

Related to 'Adh Dhira' (Lion's pawn)
Of Arab Manzil
'Geminorium'of Greeks
And 'Tsing' of Chinese Sieu

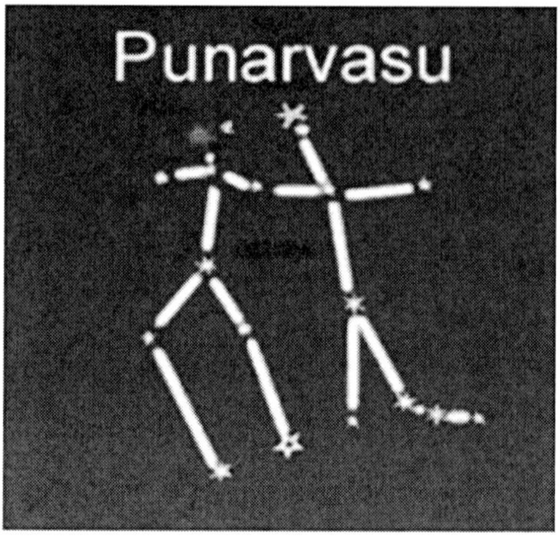

Lies Punarvasu, seventh in extension
Second chances and events' repetition;
Resilience it portends
And rising from the ashes

Daughter of Daksha
The governing deity is Aditi
And the planet Jupiter
The mother of all Gods
The infinity
Lord Ram was born too
In this Nakshtra
And so shall the owners be
Tall, oblong faced, handsome
Religious, god fearing and
Righteous shall he be

A good teacher, orator, writer
Physician, actor
The owner shall worship his parents

And destiny shall bring late
The fortune and success in life
And he may face vagaries of fate

The native shall denounce its partner
Or bitter shall be the tale
Of their relations
If family life doesn't completely fail
And mental strife and urine problems
Diabetes and anaemia shall inflict the subject
So the subject should worship
Lakshmi, Durga or Saraswati
Or jupiter and chant the mool mantra
"Om" or "Aum" 108 times

Pushya-VIII

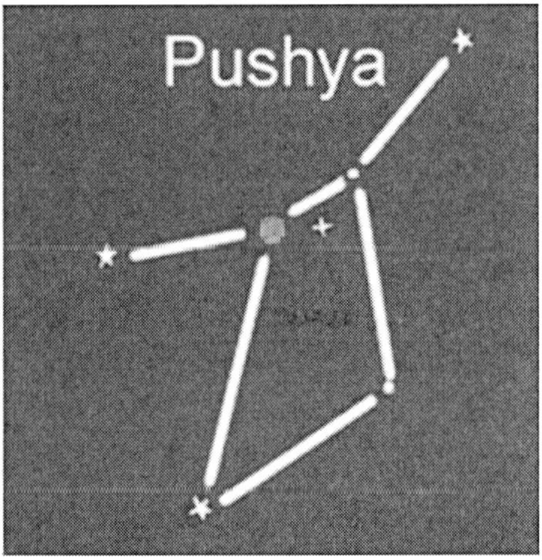

Known as 'An Nathra' (the nose gap of lion)
In Arab Manzil
'Cancri' of the Greeks

Or 'Kuei' of the Chinese Sieu
Pushya comprises of three stars
Meaning the one who nourishes
Or auspicious
Governed by 'Guru'
Or 'Brahaspathi', (Jupiter)
The teacher of Gods
And the planet Saturn
To Pushya was born Bharat
The younger brother of Ram

Born under Pushya
Ill fated shall be one
A pauper in the early life
For the parents health
Uncles, relatives and wealth

Varied in constitution
The owner shall bear a mark,
A mole or scar on face
Inconclusive in decision
Doubtful of character
Fond of clothes and
Selfishness shall one embrace

Not sure about one's capability
Shall choose the wrong options
And lead a hurdled life
With struggle and strife
In career shall opt
For teaching, dairy, merchant ship
Politics, management, psychotherapy or estate

The native shall be down
With ulcer, eczema, stone
Cancer, cough and sugar
And should worship the Mother Goddess or Hanuman
To alleviate the affliction
And chant the mool mantra
"Om Kam" 108 times

Ashlesha-IX

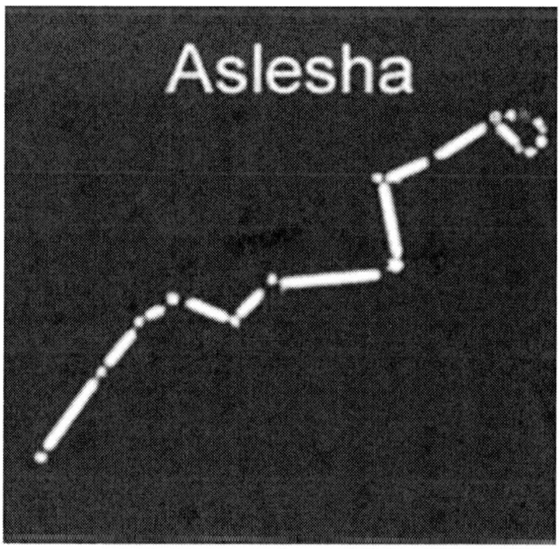

Known as 'At – Tarf'
(a look of lion) in Arab Manzil
' Hydarae' in Greek
' Lieeu' in Chinese
Ashlesha, serpentine in shape
Is a group of stars five or six
It stands for embrace
Or oneness between the two with grace

Governed by ' Naga' the Serpent
And the planet Mercury
The incarnate of Balram
In Ashlesha were born
Laxman and Shatrughan
The younger brothers of Lord Ram

Sharp in sight
Uncouth in behavior
Stout might one grow
Thankless, deceitful, shrewd, coward
Hypocrite one shall be
And organizing skill shall show

In career the subject shall go
For chemical engineering, druggist
Anaesthetist, psychiatrist, petroleum
Allopathic surgeons, tantric, shaman
Teaching, yoga and intelligence
Poor in health
Jaundice, leg problems,
Stomach disorders, urinary problems
And addiction to drugs shall one show
To avoid the troubles
The subject should worship the Snake or Lord Shiva
And chant the mool mantra
"Om Kham" and "Om Gam" 108 times

Magha – X

Magha, a group of five or six stars
Is tenth in extension

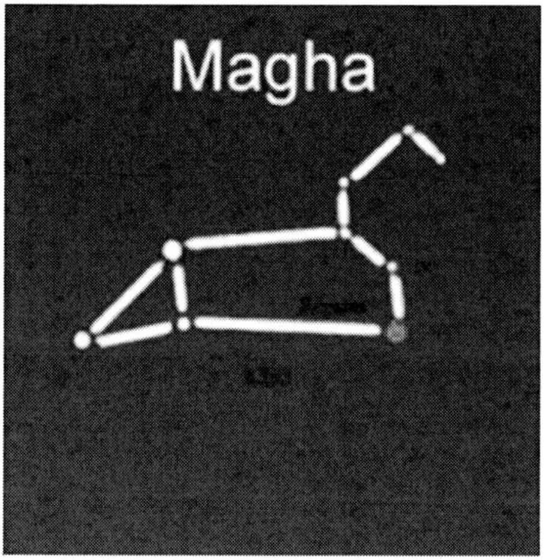

And related to 'Aj-Jabah' of Arab Manzil
'Sing' of Chinese Sieu and
'Regulas' of the Greeks
Magha governed by 'Pitra' (manes)
And the planet Ketu
Means 'mighty' or big

Medium in height
Quite hardworking are the natives
Innocent in countenance
With prominent cheeks and hairy body
Caring for the parents and relatives

Artist shall he be
And master of arts and sciences
Recognized by scholars
And humble in speech
And god fearing and full of gaiety.
Sensitive to others and social in behavior
For truth shall he stand

No place for enemies and hurdles
Away shall they strand

In career the subjects shall join
Research, administration
Judiciary, management, politics
Engineering or museums
Epilepsy, fever, night blindness
Asthma and cancer are the diseases
That afflict the subject
So the native should worship Lord Shiva
Or the Goddess Kali
And chant the mool mantra
"Om Gham" and "Om Ngam" 108 times

Purva Phalguni-XI

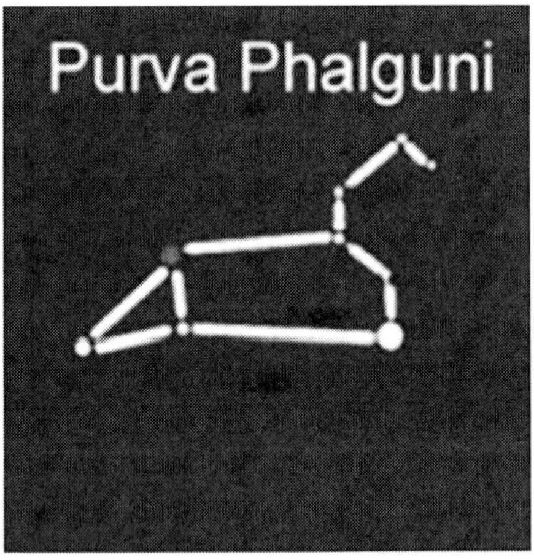

'Az-Zubrah' of Arab
'Leonis' of the Greeks
And ' Chang' of the Chinese Sieu

Purva Phalguni is a group of four stars
Like the four poles of a bed
A platform of conjugation

Governed by 'Bhaga' a son of Aditi
And the planet Venus
Symbol of Shivlingam
Or swimming hammock
The native is handsome, attractive
Robust in built
Master of many sciences
And bears qualities intuitive

Arrogant in attitude
Inimical to slavery
Frequently shall he change job,
The native shall show free will
Sincere in work, honest he shall
Bring domineering to a standstill

In career the native may become
Diplomat, politician, bureaucrat
Musician, artist, teacher and designer

He shall lead a good married life
Happiness shall flow to him
His health shall be fine
With sometime a dental problem,
Disturbed stomach and diabetes
The subject should worship
The goddess Lakshmi
And Kuber or Lord Shiva

And chant the mool mantra
"Om Cham" 108 times

Uttra Phalguni – XII

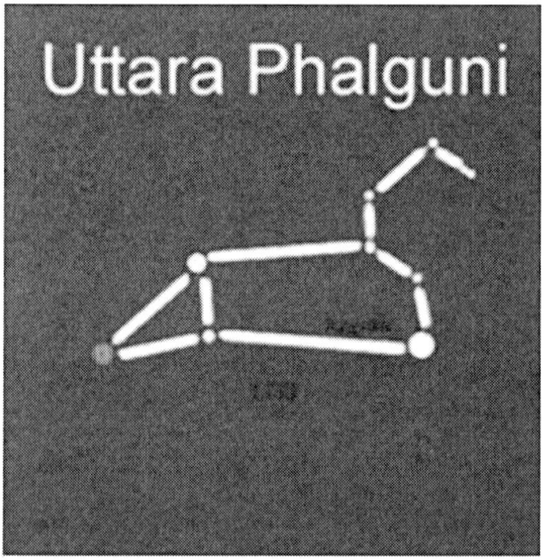

Related to 'Al-Sarfah' in Arab Manzil
'Y 'of the Chinese Sieu
And 'Lionis' of the Greeks
Uttra Phalguni has two stars
Resembling two poles in a room
Aryaman, third son of Aditi
Governs the nakshtra
And the planet Sun
A close companion, protector of mares
A play fellow or 'mitra'

The native is tall in stature
Heavy in trail
Oblong his face and parrot nose

Walks like an imposing male
Quite social in behaviour
Sincere in work, religious minded
And adamant in decision
Impatient and wrathful at time
Completes his work with precision

Teacher, researcher, scientist, writer
The native can become
Career shall blossom late
And the progress of happiness in life
Shall be slow and cumbersome

In health shall have
The native of Purva Phalguni
No special challenge in life
May rise to higher echelons
Without much struggle and strife
The subjects should worship the Sun
Chant the Gayatri mantra
And the mool mantra
"Om Chham" and "Om Im" 108 times

Hasta-XIII

'Chin' of Chinese
'Corvi' of the Greeks
And 'Al- Auwa'(the barking dog)
Of Arab Manzil
Stands Hasta at number thirteen
A group of stars five
Governed by Aditya (Sun)

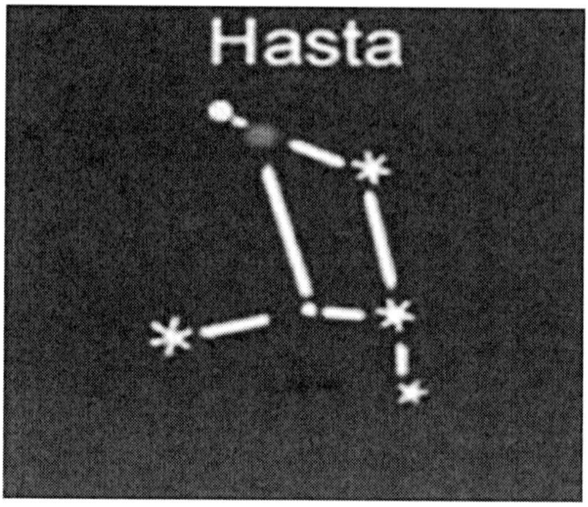

A son of Aditi
And the planet Moon
Like fingers five or hand does it thrive

Medium in stature
Stout and smart his demeanour
The native shall have no dissention
Committed to promise, selfless, honest
Calm, polite, humble in behaviour
Shall command wide attention.

Jack of all the trades
And multifarious in knowledge shall the native be
Not addicted to subordination
Promising and sincere in work
Wavering in career
And unstable the profession
Artist, poet, writer
Teacher, palmist, astrologer
Manager, accountant, designer
Decorator, agricultural engineer

For the subject are the career

Cough, fever, cold
Asthma and Cygnus are the ails
Married life quite lively
The native shall sail
The subjects of Hastha should worship the Sun
And chant the mool mantra
"Om Jham" and "Om Nyam" 108 times

Chitra-XIV

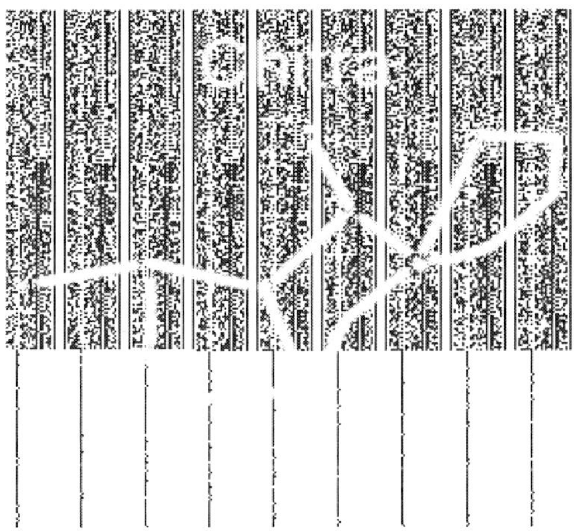

'As – Simak' of the Arab Manzil
' Virginis' of the Greeks
' Kio' of the Chinese Sieu
Is Chitra, the brilliant
Another celestial member
The pearl like star
The star of prosperity and happiness
The nakshtra fourteenth in number

Governed by Brahma
The architect or 'Tvashtav'
And the planet Mars
Creative shall the native be
Frail in body, but tall at time
Identifiable from a crowd of people
Because of virtues prime

The native shall have normal education
Hurdles and hiccups many
But blessed with intuition divine
And farsightedness
Shall have predicting power uncanny

They can be tutors, astrologers
Teachers, shamans, priest
Architects, craftsmen, fashion designers
Photographers, writers, directors
Painters, surgeons, sculptors at once
The ailments of bladder, kidney
Stomach have been noticed

To escape from the afflictions
The subject should worship mother Durga
And chant the mool mantra
"Om Tam" and "Om Tham" 108 times

Swati-XV

Fifteenth in zodiacal extension
Is Swati
Called 'Al-Gafar' in Arab Manzil

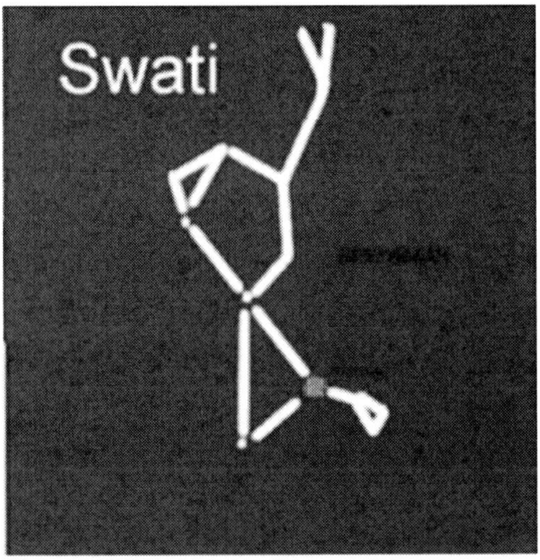

'Bootis' in Greek
Or 'King' in Chinese Sieu
It consists of one star
And Swati, means sword
For some even outcaste
The planet of the nakshtra is Rahu
And Vayu is the lord
The God of wind
The father of Bhima

Moderate in size
Fatty in flesh the native,
Lover of peace and liberty
Adamant, furious in rage
Excels in knowledge
Weak in income
Will prosper after 25 years of age

The Venusian profession

Suits one such as acting, drama, movie,
Gold smithery, engineering, fashion
Drug selling, travel, teaching
Pilot, sports, law

Good in health,
And marital status
But arthritis, heart and abdomen
May overpower the subject
In determination for others Afflatus
So the native should adore
Mother Sarswati to alleviate the ills
And chant the mool mantra
"Om Lam", "Om Am"
"Om Ksham" and "Om Aam" 108 times

Vishakha-XVI

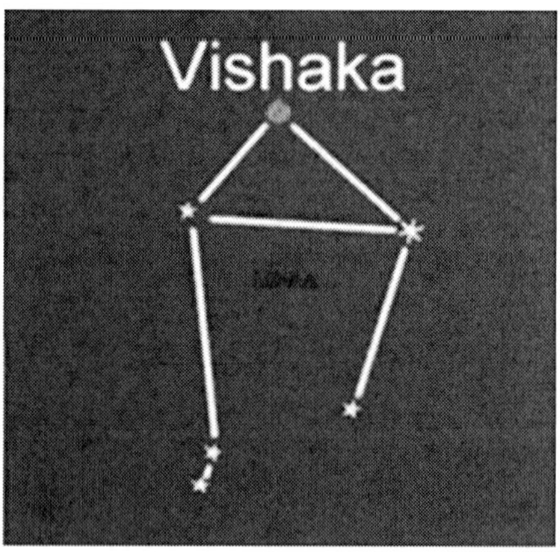

'Az-Zumanan' (Arms of Scorpio) in Arab
'Librae' of Greeks
And 'Ti' of China

Is Vishakha , the group for stars four
For some just two
Looks like a potter's wheel

The ruling planet is Jupiter
And the deity Indra and Agni
The lords of senses, sacrifice and desire
A mixture of height
Fat and lean in stature
Round shall be the face
In appearance charming and dear
Attractive in features
Shall sparkle in public sphere

He should join politics, banking
Or teaching, consultancy, modelling
Broadcasting, forces, customs as career
Victorious in debates, eloquence
Sharp in wit
And agile in action
Master of word deliverance

The native shall be reckless in love
And profligate in life
To balance the nature's vitality
Fond of drinks and drugs even
Shall bring happiness to the family

In health the native is prone to nerves
And problems of nervous crackdown
Sprains and injuries in feet
The crutches in arms shall stall a while

And may keep the native down
So Hari-Hara, eight Vasus
The subject should worship
And chant 108 times the mantra
" Om Yam" and " Om Ram"

Anuradha - XVII

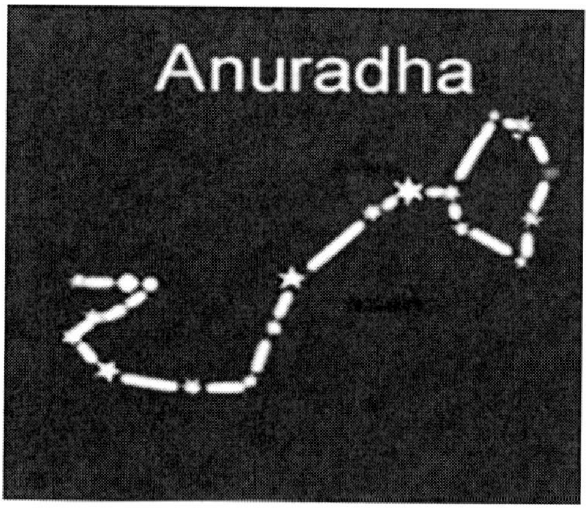

In Arab Manzil known as 'Al-Iklil' (the crown)
In China as 'Fang'
And 'Scorpion' in Greek
Anuradha nakshtra is seventeenth in count
It has three stars
Which mean success
And rise in life paramount

Governed by the planet Saturn
And the deity Mitra
A son of Aditi
That stands for mind and hair
The cerebral cells are the

Representatives of grain, grass
And the intellectual affairs

In the native of Anuradha
The contrast of beauty and vain exists
Charming face, large eyes
If Ill aspected by planets
Then ugliness shall persist

Perseverance in works
In attitude quite vindictive
Lack of peace and happiness
Shall flow towards the native
Good in education
And fields of commerce
The native shall go for business
The early cracker of the work and job
The obstacles many shall handle with grace

In career the native may join
Music, teaching, foreign travels
Astrology, intelligence, research
Diplomats, industry etc
And may go down
With severe pains, headache
Cough, constipation
Fever, burns and cyclic disorders
The Anuradha native should worship Sun
The 12 Adityas, and chant the moola mantra
"Om Am" and "Om Im" 108 times

Jyeshtha-XVIII

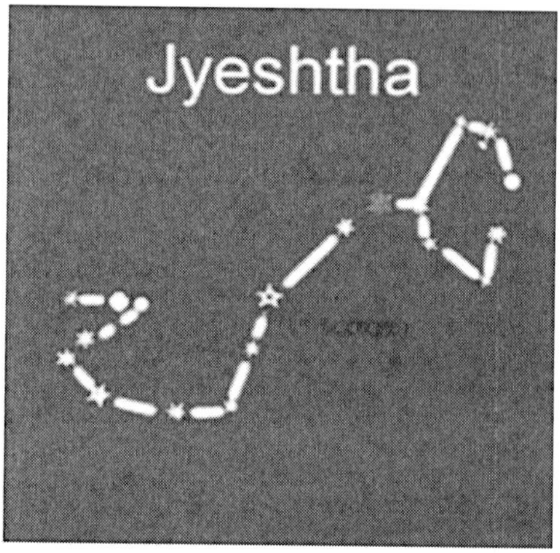

Jyeshtha, eighteenth in number
Stands for elder, the larger
And is known as 'Al-Katab' in Arab Manzil
'Antares' in Greek
'Sin' in Chinese
Is a group of stars three
Hangs like a pendent
Brightening, alluring shining free

Indra, the native of Amrawati
The destroyer of hundred forts
Lord of rains and storms
The architect is the ruler of Jyeshtha
And Mercury the planet

Stout in constitution the native
Full of vitality and vigour
Charming countenance

Bulging teeth or dental flaws
Yet unique seem in figure
Disliked by kin and relatives
He would have friction at home
In altercation domestic
To wife remains subservient

The native will have to struggle a lot
Free from shelter at home
Shall lead a lonely life away with
Forces, bureaucracy, broadcasting
Sports, navy, management
Intelligence, trade and acting as career
In health may have
Dysentery, fever, cough, stomach
Restlessness, insomnia
Sincere at heart and labours at work
The native shall earn name
But obstinacy and ill temperament
Shall bring more defame

To alleviate the ill influences
The native should worship Lord Vishnu
Or Durga and Kali
And chant the mool mantra
"Om Dham" 108 times

Moola – XIX

'Ash-Shaulah' (scorpion's bite) in Arab
' Scorpionis' in Greek
And ' Uei' in China

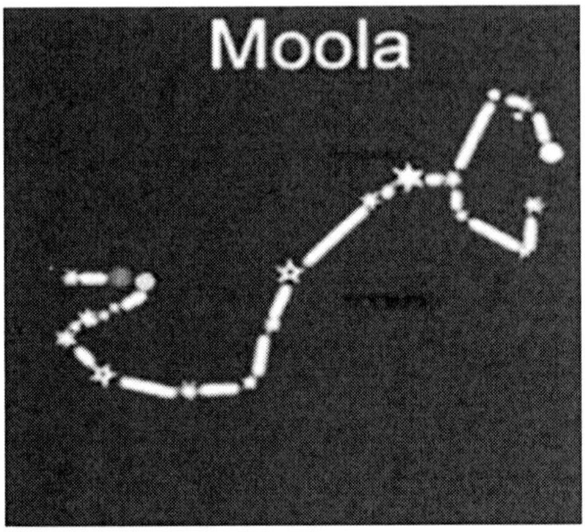

Is the Nakshtra Moola
A group of stars nine
For some a couple it is
Also called 'Vicrtau'
Or two releasers in Athrva Veda
That exonerates one from pain
When in ascendance

Ketu is the ruling Planet of Moola
And the deity is Nirriti
The goddess with golden locks
Of the realms of hidden sorrows
And death, related with Dhumavati
One of the aspects of Kali
Rules Moola, the root or origin that means

The native has bright wide eyes
Handsome shape and stature,
Charming countenance
Attractive features
Peace loving, principled in life

Upholding value in his intrinsic nature

He shall master many fields
And unstable in profession will be
A good adviser in finance and business
At distant places shall he work
In careers such as forces, medicines
Surgery, politics, petroleum, mortician
Intelligence, judiciary and research

The native may undergo ill fate and distress
Tuberculosis, stomach or nervous disorder
Skin, scurvy and paralysis
Shall he contest in life

So Lord Shiva or Kali should one worship
And chant the mantra 108 times
" Om Pham" and " Om Pam"

Poorva Ashadha-XX

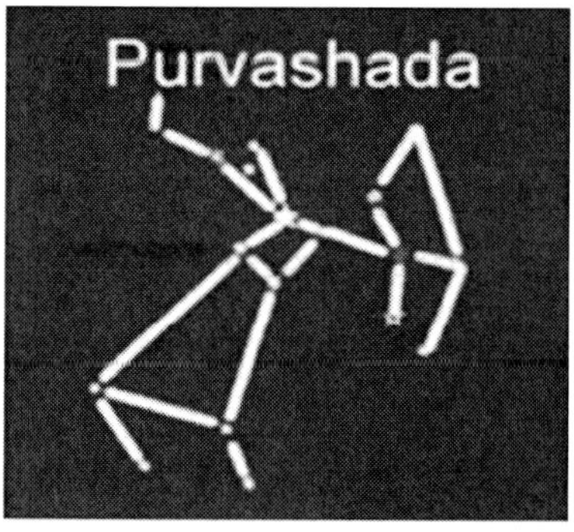

Poorva Ashadha corresponds to 'Sagittari' of Greeks
'Ki' of Chinese Sieu

And ' An-Naaim' of Arab
Meaning 'formerly unsubdued'
Venus governs the nakshtra
Or the 'Jal' (water) is deity
A group of four stars
Appears like a tusk mighty

Tall in stature
Bright eyes, lean and slim frame
Pomegranate teeth
The native is resplendent in outlook
Debater, decisive, sharp in wit
Indomitable, recalcitrant
Even if on in the wrong side
Ideas in his mind flow like a brook

God fearing, religious, benevolent
Writer, poet shall be the native
For profession can be surgeon
In fine art, writing, accounts
May be a figure prominent
And the years from 30 to 50 shall
Happen to be important
From brothers, parents shall he gain
With partner relations average
And live in land foreign

In health the lungs are weak
Bronchial illness, breathing problems
Jaundice, tuberculosis and heart
Fever, infections shall wreak
Severe illness

Therefore, the native should worship
Goddess Laxmi and chant the mantra
" Om Bam" 108 times

Uttar Ashadha-XXI

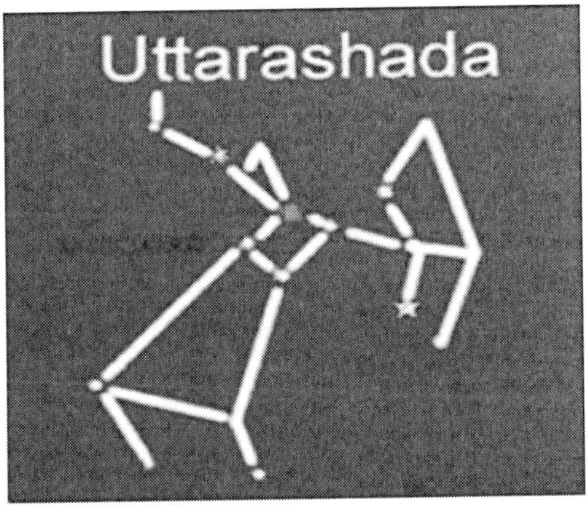

The next in number is Uttar Ashadha
Called 'Saggitarii' in Greek
'Teu' in Chinese
And 'Al-Baldah' in Arab Manzil.
Quite opposite to Poorva,
Uttar means later
And Ashadh 'unsubdued'
With stars four in form
The nakshtra looks like a table
Or four legged platform

Governed by ten Visvadevas
(collective gods)
And the planet Sun
In constitution tall shall be the native

Long nose, deep eyes and broad head
Bright face and attractive looks
Like an impressive doyen shall he spread

God fearing, simple in nature
Far from pomp and glory
Shall the native be
Pure heart and soft at tongue
Straight forward, sincere
And to some extent a slave to flattery.
Like Poorva Ashadha
His education shall be balanced
And the native may join
Teaching, priesthood, astrology
Bureaucracy, medicines, sports
Construction, politics and engineering
In health poor eyesight, neurotic disorder
Abdominal aches shall overwhelm the native
So one should worship
Lord Ganesha, the obstacle remover
And chant mantra
" Om Bham" and " Om Bha" 108 times

Abhijit – XXII

'Sa'd- Adh-Dhabih' in Arab
'Vega' of the Greeks
And 'Nieu' of Chinese
Is the nakshtra Abhijit
Governed by Brahma
The Lord of creation

One born in 'Abhijit muhurta'
Half an hour before
And after mid night and mid day
Like Krishna shall have great fortunes
Invincible shall he be
And attractive in countenance
Medium statured
A doyen in speech and deliverance

Extremely humble and respectful
To one and all
A highly learned scholar, master of art
Teacher, lawyer, priest and business
He domineers, towering above all
In intellect and arenas where others seem small.

Though counted not among nakshtras by many
Abhijit still carries weight
Brings early marriage
Abundance in family and prosperity

The native may be orator, teacher, guide
Philosopher, strategician, scholar
Warrior, politician and martial
Some early troubles in health
Like jaundice and infections
The life shall move at a majestic gait
The native should worship Vishnu
And chant the mantra
" Om Namo Bhagwate Vasudevay Namah"

Shravan-XXIII

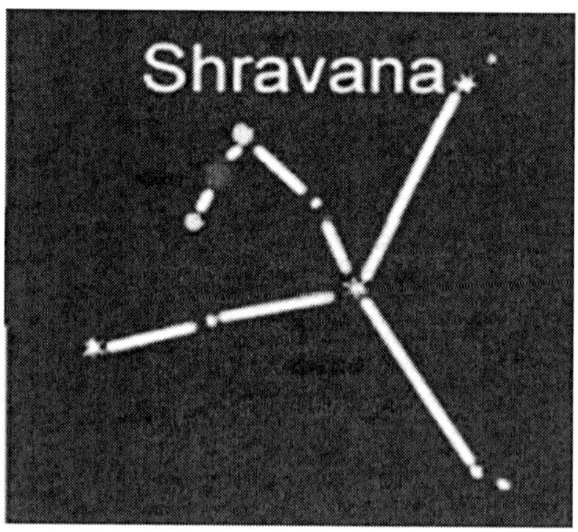

Sharavan is twenty third in number
Meaning to hear, is comprised of stars three
Referred to as 'Aquarri'in Greek
'Al-bula'(devourer) in Arab
And 'Nu'in Chienese Sieu
In growth and prowess like a higher tree

Ruled by the planet Moon and
Governed by Vishnu

The lord of progress
Of highest order
In prowess and knowledge
The nakshtra of mother Sharda too

Charming in look
Short in stature
Some mole on face or shoulder
The native is firm and mature.
Truthful in voice
Firm in character and gaze
A life of values he leads
Neat in appearance calm at mind
The disorder shall he raze

Teacher, linguist; guide
Artist, poet, columnists
A good organizer or psychologists
Shaman doctor can one be
Shall have the best partner in life
And happiness in every sphere

On health front the native shall remain
Largely good and sturdy
But may be gripped
By eczema, rheumatism
Stomach disorder and skin issues
So one should worship the Lord Vishnu
And chant the mantra
" Om Mam" 108 times

Dhanishtha – XXIV

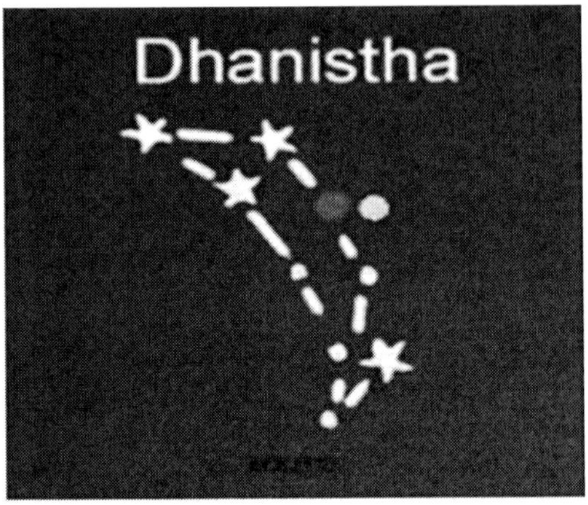

'Sa'd-as-Suud' (quite felicitous) in Arab Manzil
'Hiu' in Chinese
And 'Capricornii' of the Greeks
Is Dhashishtha, meaning the fortunate or famous.
Comprises of four stars
In the shape of a drum
The Dhanishtha nakshtra is ruled
By the planet Mars
And the eight Vedic deities
'Asht Vasavs'
Apah (music), Druva (perseverance),
Dhara (wisdom), Anila (commerce),
Anala (energy), Pratyusha (joy and hope)
Prabhasa (good nature) and Soma (sensitivity)
Believed to have originated from Ganga

The Dhanishtha born
Are lean in constitution mostly
And master of many sciences

Learned scholars and connoisseur
Secretive in opinion, patient listeners
And vindictive in nature

The blessings of lords eight
Make Dhanishtha born quite wise
Who can be a poet, musician, artist
Doctor, engineer, shaman
Astrologer, soldier, shaman
Surgeon, artist and many more
The performer of levels great

Cough, infection and abdominal disorder
Are the issues in health
Therefore, the native should adore
The Goddess Durga or Lord Vishnu
To alleviate the illness
And chant the mool mantra
" Om Yam" and " Om Ram" 108 times

Satabhisha-XXV

Meaning a hundred healers (physicians)
Satabhisha is twenty fifth in zodiac extension
Comprises of stars hundred
Only one star Khanda-Katak mentions

Known as 'Sad- al-Melic'
(lucky one for king) in Arab
'Aquarri' of the Greeks
And 'Goei' of the Chinese Sieu
Satabhisha is ruled by planet Rahu

And the deity Varun
The God of rain, the cosmic water

The native normally shall have
Frail and soft body
Attractive countenance, rising nose
A look of the noble aristocrat
Sharp wit and memory
The flambeau of truth
The native shall bear
For truth shall lay his life
Sincere, hardworking, efficient in work
The early life flogged with strife

An artist, a poet or a literary figure
Of prominence the native shall rise
Astronaut, researcher, teacher
Engineer, pilot, scientist
Writer, druggist, guru
Yoga practitioner

His career may comprise

In health asthma, bronchitis
Diabetes, urinary problems
And poor immunity may take place
But worshipping of lord Shiva
And chanting of mool mantra
" Om Lam" 108 times
May bring peace and solace

Poorva-Bhadrapad-XXVI

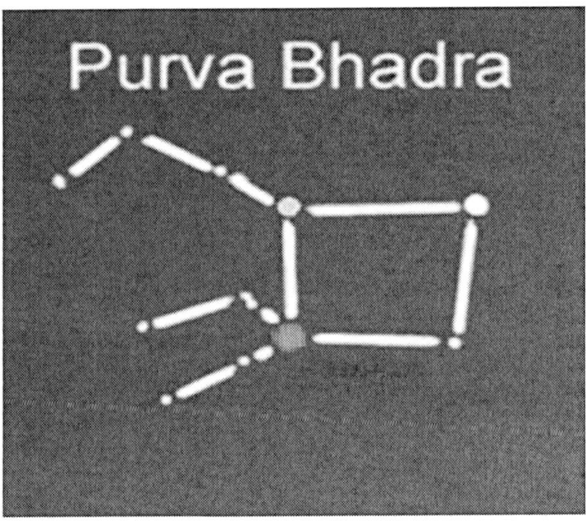

'Al-Fargah-Al-Mukdim'(four spouts of water jar)
in Arab Manzil
'Pegasi' of the Greeks
And 'Che' of the Chinese
Is the Poorva-Bhadrapad
Comprising of two
Couch like stars

Meaning extremely beautiful
Or 'former with lucky feet'

Ruled by planet Jupiter
And the deity Aj Ekpad
A one legged snake
Or a form of Rudra or Shiva
The native of the nakshtra are
Simple and peace lovers
Sensitive, sincere and indolent
Yet intelligent and good at trade

Strange shall be the jobs of the native
like morticians, surgeons
Occultist, astrologer
Pharmaceuticals, industry, fire and police
In health paralysis, diabetes and infection
May befall the native
Should worship lord Shiva or hanuman
And chant the mantra
"Om Vam" and "Om Sham" 108

Uttara-Bhadrapad-XXVII

Uttara Bhadrapad is twenty seventh
In zodiacal extension
In Arab Manzil as 'Al-Parag-Al-Mukhir'
'Pi' in Chinese
And 'Andromedae' in Greek
Has got the mention

The nakshtra comprises of two stars

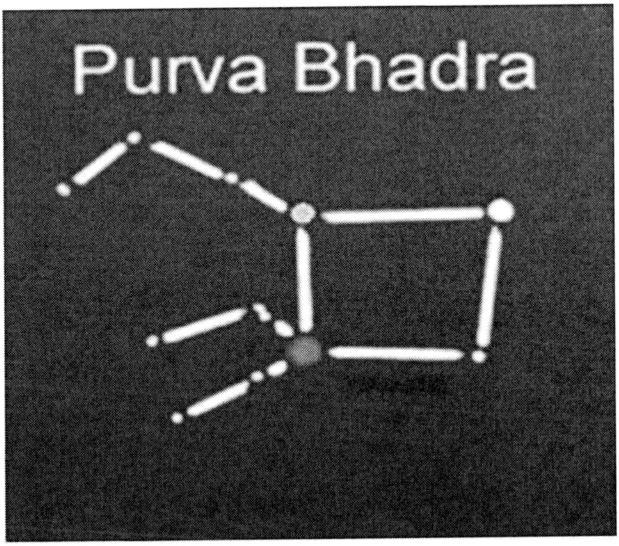

Pegasus and Andromeda
Like the legs of the bed
Governed by planet Saturn
And the deity mythical Ahir Budhnya
The snake or serpent of the deep sea
An auspicious serpent or naga
Associated with Shiva's army
Makes the native a warrior

The nakshtra consists of two bright stars,
Imposing personality
Impressive looks and heart warm
At first sight is the beholder enslaved
With the magnetic charm
Egalitarian eye
An angel to friends and fear to foe
In one instance for friends the native
His life can bestow

Well educated and learned
Shall be the native
Multifaceted in knowledge
Yoga guide, teacher, Counsellor, therapist
Shaman, Tantric, Researcher
Poetry, Music and Art
Come naturally to his share
Piles, hernia and nervous ailments
May his health ensnare
So native should worship
Lord Shiva, mother Durga or Lord Vishnu
And chant the mool mantra
" Om Sham" and " Om Sam"

Revati-XXVIII

Last in number is Revati nakshtra
Comprising of stars thirty two
Shaping a drum
Called 'Piscium' in Greek
'Koei' in Chinese and
'Batn-al-Hut'(the fish's belly) in Arab Manzil
Meaning wealthy or prosperous
Governed by Pushan
The nourishing Lord
The journey, from this world into the next

Fair in look and moderate in height
Clean at heart sincere in work
Free in life shall be native
Orthodox in nature
Superstitious and hasty

Spiteful but close of the relatives

Shall have education great
Science, history, research, archaeology
Astrology and stars in range
Artist, musician, actor, entertainer
Linguist, astrologer, police,
Businessman can the native be
Dental defects, ulcer, abdominal disorders
May occur to one
So the worship of Vishnu is imminent
And the chanting of Mantra
"Om Lam" and "Om Ksham" 108 times
When the moon transits Revati nakshatra
To minimise the impact
And keep health intact

References

Raghunandan Prasad Gaur, *Nakshtra Jyotish*, Manoj Books, Delhi.

K. T. Shubhakaran, *Nakshtra (Constellation) Based Preditions*, New delhi, Sagar Publications, 1991.

http://wantastro.blogspot.in/2014/03/uttara-bhadrapada-nakshatra-in-astrology.html

https://hi.wikipedia.org/wiki/

CHAPTER 3

Planetary Properties

SOM P RANCHAN AND HARISH K THAKUR

Sun

The previous chapters dealt essentially with zodiac signs, planets, their affinities and disinclinations vis-à-vis one another, the power of the combinations in houses and signs in human affairs and destinies. This chapter now will focus on the planets.

Needless to say that any description of the planets should begin with the Sun, the chief star that governs our universe. The Sun represents one's cardinal personality, burning bright and resplendent. It represents the spirit, the demi-urge (in the platonic sense).

Since the Sun is essential for humans to see and is also symbolic of light, the Gyana i.e. knowledge, it represents eye and soul. Since it is fire and fire is essential for digestion, it represents the stomach and the fire in the heart. In so far as it is indestructible, it represents bone in man. In symbolic language, Sun is *Vajra*.

In the external collective in society, culture, history, Sun naturally will represent power of the state, government. For family dynamics it represents the father principle, even though the principle may be under challenge these days. Sun represents the aggression of the warrior who puts his enemies to flight. Thakur writes:

> Sun, the almighty
> Represents the Lagna
> The personality
> The fire inside, the vanity
>
> It represents the soul
> The fire, crimson, copper
> Sun is father, the state, the reign
> In exaltation goes berserk
> In triangle or house number ten
> And no one can restrain it
> From the throw of prowess
> That flows from its arms
> When the enemy it aggresses

So far we have dealt with the powers of the Sun. Essentially, the Sun has been seen factually and archetypally. The power of the Sun is at its best in the tenth house, which is the house of one's profession, career or *karmasthana*. It is through one's profession that one earns name and fame in the community. The same is true in case the exalted or good sun is placed in the Lagna house. If well aspected sun is placed in the eleventh house one wins the grace of state (elevation to high state echelons) and also enjoys the pleasure of vehicle quite early in life. Its placement in the third and sixth house is though, problematic for brothers and sisters yet makes one valorous and brings enemies to their knees.

In combination with Rahu and Saturn or aspected therefrom, sun becomes malefic. When malefic it becomes vain, overbearing, hot. Rahu is regarded as a shadow planet. When afflicted with bad Rahu its lustre is dimmed. It uses its powers for ill purposes. It invites ignominy. Since as was pointed out earlier that it governs sight, heart, stomach these organs run into problems.

It is believed (Jatak Parijat, Bhrigusanhita and others) that in such cases offering of *Argha* with water to Sun every morning brings solace. The other means of pleasing the planet are fasting on Sunday and donating brown or copper coloured grains, clothing or metal.

The weak or the problematic Sun should be appeased and propitiated with the wearing of *Ruby* in a ring in the index finger or a locket. Even Patanjali too recommended the use of stones and gems as they reflect frequencies of light in which we have our being. The best remedy is chanting of Bij Mantra of Sun in the morning. The true pronunciation, of course needs to be clarified before going for it.

Bij Mantra : *Aum Hram Hrim Hraom Sah Suryayah Namah*

सूर्य तांत्रिक मंत्र : *ॐ ह्रां ह्रीं ह्रौं सः सूर्याय नमः।*

Moon

From the Sun we come to the moon. Why the moon, skipping heavier planets like the Saturn, Jupiter, Venus, Mars. The reason is simple. The moon is closest to us, the terrestrial beings. Even Sun's power comes into us, mediating, reflected through the moon. Without the moon as intermediary, no life would be possible on the planet earth.

So moon becomes our consciousness, our mind, in so far as consciousness is in the body, moon is the reality of the body entire. So moon represents the psyche and the body.

Together with the Sun, it represents Pneuma, Psyche, Harish Thakur writes:

> Though small in size
> But its short distance from earth
> Maximizes
> The impact of moon
> Over the life
> Of man, creatures and mind
> Moon is water,
> Moon is wave,
> Moon is emotion,
> It makes the heart kind

In life we see that relationally we are closer to woman, who is just experienced as mother, later includes sister, wife, daughter. So moon is the spectrum of the feminine for both men and women. Rudrabhat also says that, if Sun is king then Moon is queen and the duo represents the soul and the mind.

In so far as moon is consciousness as postulated earlier, it will give us ease and facility with arts and letters. The moon waxes and wanes. The waxing moon gives us emotional vibrancy, passion and joyance. The waning moon lowers bios.

Shadowed by Rahu and Saturn, Moon poses problems because, it cannot withstand like the Sun can. It opens itself to blood pressure, odema, gynae infections, mental ailments and jaundice. Psychologically, it opens the door to hallucinations, instability.

Astrologers recommend fasting on Monday and wearing a *pearl stone*. Donation of rice, silver or white cloth is recommended. Monday is attributed to Lord Shiva, the sovereign spirit in Indian mythology. Naturally in the periods of low, depleted physical energy and psychic entropy, one has to resort to the Gnostic spirit, call upon the Sun to energize one and charge the physical and psychic batteries.

Bij Mantra : *Aum Shram Shrim Shrom Sah Chandramase Namah*

सूर्य तांत्रिक मंत्र : *'ॐ श्रां श्रीं श्रौं सः चन्द्रमसे नमः'।*

Mercury

Since, we have dealt with the moon closest to the earth, it is but natural that we should deal now with mercury, which is closest to the Sun. In fact, it is a nano fragment of the Sun, which orbits around it. It completes its passage around Sun in 88 days.

In astrology it is shown as being with the Sun, a bit before or after in the house where the Sun is. When it is with the Sun (within the range of 5 degree on either side) many believe that it is combusted. This means that it is *ast* or has no independent existence or significance in influencing the native.

However, according to another theory all the planets close to the Sun (within 5 degree range on either side) combust except Mercury. Saint Prashar is also of the view that mercury is too bright and mercurial to lose its impact.

When it is placed in a house before the house of Sun, it shows the ability to reflect on what the Sun is doing. It has the power to correct when it falls before Sun. It should be considered as a ground breaker, pathfinder. It is a teeny-weeny Prometheus. Speaking imagistically, if Sun be the dragon of Light and fire, it is a nano mouse hurrying scurrying, colonizing, restless, up and doing.

Its quality of anticipating the things ahead of course makes it a foreteller. The charts of most of the foretellers verify the fact as most of them have good Mercury preceding the house of Sun.

The debilitated Mercury can hassle the tongue and cause lukederma. It also causes neuro problems and skin burns, if joined by exalted sun. It also affects throat, nasal, lungs, intestines and kidneys in case of ill aspects of malefic.

In Western psychology cum astrology the planet Mercury is valued highly. Together with Saturn, it unfolds the powers of the self, makes for *Prapti* and *Sakamya* giving one's powers and capacities to do things for others. Powerful and fluent is the spirit in us. Unfortunately, in Indian astrology mercury is not valourized as it should be.

Bij Mantra : *Aum Bram Brim Braum Sah Budhay Namah.*

बुध मंत्र : 'ॐ ब्रां ब्रीं ब्रौं सः बुधाय नमः।

Saturn

Like Mercury, Saturn too is valued less in the Indian folk psychology and astrology. Because, it is far in the planetary scheme, it is seen as intrusive which in fact is not. It is the demesne of the archetypes, being at the edge of the empyrean.

It is a known fact that archetypal energies when not assimilated, they make for discordance. So when Saturn is right, it makes for longevity, wealth, name, triumph over obstacles and snags. Engineers, builders, contractors, brokers, property dealers and surgeons all have an element of Saturn, without which their fate can never take due turn.

People are mostly scared of the approach of Saturn in their charts because of certain myths. It is believed that Saturn brings ill fate and problems in life. This is because of juridical posture of Saturn. It punishes the evil doer and blesses the honest and hardworking. Thakur writes:

Saturn is skeleton weak and old
Lazarus, lame, king of darkness
Oblique in aspect, unforgiving
Gives mass following great
Judge and the law ultimate

In dark robe shall he march
From brightness, sun and moon
With all worldly passion
Against the wisdom of Jupiter
Divinity of Uranus,
Not in expansion but in recession
To the abyss infinite

Since, people mostly are engaged in this or that kind of pilfering, they are penalized by Saturn. Consequently, they attribute hostility to Saturn whereas, in fact Saturn is known for honesty, hard work, and steadiness in life. The latter need not worry about the Saturn's ascribed bad image.

On the negative side, the poorly placed Saturn makes for suspiciousness, over cautiousness, sluggishness, non-action. It is regarded as enemy to the Sun, though it happens to be son of the planet Sun. Mythlogically, it is seen as Shiva's son also who afflicts the great God as a shadow.

It is also said to be the bestower of long term diseases, misfortunes and death. Malefic Saturn can be causative of life or degradation of the house, it is placed in. A debilitated Saturn in the fourth house is bad for mother, in the ninth or tenth house for father or profession, in the seventh for partner, in eleventh for income or elder brother and in the eighth for self and so on.

Yet, Saturn is Venus' friend and if it is Venus' friend, it cannot be that bad. Perhaps, it gives to Venus known for passion certain clarity.

Unfortunately, Saturn is viewed as black, despite its sixteen moons and its size.

Bij Mantra : *Aum Pram Prim Prom Sah Shaneshchray (Shanaye) Namah.*

शनि मंत्र : ॐ प्रां प्रीं प्रौं सः शनये नमः।

Jupiter

Now we take Jupiter, Mars and Venus. Jupiter is considered as a planet that represents spirituality and knowledge. Since, physically it is 1300 times larger than earth its digbal or power to influence the native is quite high. It has radioactive bursts from time to time and is regarded as benign, wisdom's fount, *dharmic*, giver of ethics and righteousness, bestower of fortunes, name and fame in society.

Since, it looks yellow from earth it is causative of jaundice, diabetes, cholesterol, bad stomach and obesity.

Jupiter is also bestower of son, brother, husband, education, knowledge, religiosity and respect. It is responsible for the causation of first, fifth, ninth, tenth and eleventh house. Hence, the areas of self, knowledge, fate, profession and income belong to it and without doubt these are the areas of utmost importance in one's life. See the wit of Harish K Thakur:

Sun, Mars, Saturn, Venus
Among the planets all
Mind, wisdom, spirit and truth
Of Jupiter stands tall

It is colossal, mature, sturdy
Planner, guide, educator
Cool, visionary, philosopher

Seer, ascetic, and mentor

Guru the man will be
And lord of followers many
Sparkle like a sun
In the dark deeps uncanny

Of what use knowledge or property is, if you don't have the fate (you fail to reap the happiness out of them). That is why the position of Jupiter is considered of prime importance in a chart.

In charts, where Jupiter is Maarkesh (killer, owner of second or seventh house) it causes different problems as per the equations with other planets. As a Maarkesh, its relation with the fifth is causative of problems relating to conception, education and digestion; relation with third or eleventh of deafness or ear related diseases, with fourth of gas or stomach disorder and even cholesterol and with ninth of misfortunes and atheism.

To keep the Guru happy one has to give due regards to elders and older ones and of course to teachers. The donation of Laddu, chana, turmeric, yellow topaz, yellow cloth and gold is also suggested.

Bij mantra : *Aum Gram Grim Grom Sah Gurve Namah*

ॐ ग्रां ग्रीं ग्रौं सः गुरुवे नमः।

Mars

Mars as the name denotes is a fighter. Imposing shall be he in every sphere of life, especially distinguishing himself in sports, struggle and strife. Power is the mantra, karma and the tantra of Mars. It's the planet of the aggressive libido. When not channeled, might be the cause of debilitation. It is needlessly audacious, quarrelsome, foolhardy and brings into brain maladies such as boils, muscular dystrophy etc. Muscular dystrophy because it is somatotonic in that its strength inheres in the muscles. It suffers from blood pressure because it rages and rashes.

Violence is the prime virtue of Mars, if not given the proper vent. Under the influence of malefic, it has been observed that it derails one in life as it impels the bearer to become burglar, dacoit, murderer and rebel. Thakur elaborates immensely this:

Young, youthful, strong, passionate
Crimson, hot and royal is Mars
Lightening in tresses, fire in barrel
Swelling biceps, always at war

The combination of fire can cause explosions and so is expected when Mars joins hands with Sun and Ketu. The duo of Mars and Ketu causes accidents, of course, under the influence of malefic planets. The area of effect could be ascertained by the prime features of planets, houses and *bhavesh* engaged in.

It is also believed to be causative of loss of blood and blood pressure. However, in such cases the role of moon also needs to be studied.

The aspect of a malefic Saturn on mars is also believed to affect the muscular system of a person. Since Mars represents muscles and blood also, any disorder regarding the same is studied from the position of Mars in the chart. Its relation with the house number eight, it has been observed, leads to problems of hernia or testes.

The best remedy to appease the hot Mars is the worship of Mother Durga or Lord Hanuman and fasting on Tuesday. Coral is the stone and red items like red cloth or brown eatables can be donated.

Bij Mantra : *Aum Kram Krim Krom sah Bhomay namah*

भौम मंत्र : 'ॐ क्रां क्रीं क्रौं सः भौमाय नमः।

Venus

If Mars is masculine libido, Venus is feminine libido which attracts not just Mars but cast a spell on all the planets, such be its sexual energy.

Venus, the Greek goddess of love truly represents the planet. However, in Indian astrology Venus represents the Guru of Devils i.e. Shukracharya, who if pleased blesses one with wealth, luxuries, philanthropy and love of nature and beauty. Venus is the causative planet of seventh House, the house of partnership, joint ventures and trade. Hence, it has a special role in dealing with the affairs of wife, love, sex and bilateral mutuality. Thakur expresses this element wonderfully:

The queen of beauty
The queen of love
Besides courtship, marriage, sex
Venus stands far above

It is bright, illumined
As if damsel in heaven
Fire of eye
Ray of mind
Tippler's tip in tavern

It has been observed that people governed by this planet are great lovers of nature, beauty and are mostly writers, artists, actors or engaged in some creative profession. Most of the actors or people connected with film industry have Venus either in the tenth house or in Lagna or fourth. The role of Venus has been found to be of utmost importance in the career of these people.

The placement of Venus in the house number four or eleven, it is sure, gives one the happiness of vehicle. The miracles of wealth and consequently multiple luxuries are at the feet of such people.

Anything that weakens Venus leads to spoiling of the Venus related things. Its placement under the malefic planets or even the signs of venus (Libra and Taurus) under such influence might bring problems like poor health of wife, close partner, poor sperm count (weakness in conception), sex related problems and huge loss in commerce.

The combination of Venus with enemies like Jupiter also brings unhappiness in marital life. If Venus is markesh, its relation with the fifth house creates problems in conception. If joined by Mars it plays havoc to sex related acts and problematize the same.

Diamond is the stone number one for the remedy of the planet. Besides this fasting on Friday and donation of white things like silver, white cloth, sugar or rice is suggested.

Bij Mantra : *Aum Dram Darim Draum Sah Shukray Namah*

शुक्र मंत्र : 'ॐ द्रां द्रीं द्रौं सः शुकाय नमः'।

The Shadow Planets

All the planets have been dealt within the foregoing survey except Rahu and Ketu. Just as well because Rahu and Ketu are not planets. They are astronomically speaking the locales of the moon in its elliptical spin around the earth. When the Moon is farthest away from the earth, its locale is called Rahu in the northern hemisphere and Ketu in the southern hemisphere. The point which is being made is that in such situations the earth is not receiving the radiance and the sapidity in the measure it normally receives. This is deprivation of the earth.

Despite the denuding of the earth these two shadowy planets have no independent nature. In the horoscope they assume the nature of the planets they are with.

Rahu as a shadow is equated with Saturn. Why it is so, there is no explanation. Since Saturn is shadow, critically difficult, archetypically far off in space and difficult to tame and assimilate it assumes darker characteristics mythologically. Rahu would pose not too dissimilar a challenge. Since Saturn shadows the Sun, opposes light, be it of sun and moon, the fiery glow of Mars and the rocket radiance of the Venus, Rahu will do the same. So the light and the warmth bearing planets have to reduce their darkness and its critical capers. Then Rahu will become an ally, an auxiliary. Viewed thus psychologically, it will strengthen the Sun, Mars, Venus and Moon.

Now Ketu is regarded as an agent of Mars. Let us play with the images from iconography and from myth and lore. In one story he was to devour the moon. The latter takes shelter in Shiva's matted locks. Rahu implores Shiva to release him so that he can eat the moon and allay his hunger. Shiva tells him to enter his locks and make a meal of the moon. Rahu enters but his nature changes. The message is that Rahu's hunger, anger, shadow and criticality should be spiritualized. In the churning of nectar story, Rahu succeeds in licking a bit of nectar and consequently becomes semi-divine. Ketu becomes semi-divine too licking the self same nectar.

If Rahu is overvaulting, leaping head, Ketu is the headless body. If Rahu alienates because of intellectuality, Ketu recoils emotionally. Ketu in his recoil is considered to be a yogi in the making. He turns away from relationships and human ties. The recoil is aggressive.

However, both Rahu and Ketu are into collapsing cathexes. Indian astrology lately has added to its planetary mandala Uranus, Neptune and Pluto. The effort is commendable but not worthwhile because they are not really in the Bhupara, the outside surround as to have no meaningful impact on human affairs.

Bij Mantra : *Rahu* : *Aum Bhram Bhrim Bhrom Sah Rahve Namah*

राहु मंत्र : 'ॐ भ्रां भ्रीं भ्रौं सः राहवे नमः।

Ketu : Aum Stram Satrim Strom Sah Ketve Namah

केतु मंत्र : 'ॐ स्रां स्रीं स्रौं सः केतवे नमः।

CHAPTER 4

Introduction to the Zodiac

SOM P RANCHAN

Part I

Zodiac is a constellation of thousands of stars. It is a massive, mind boggling archetype which governs your life which is just a speck from one of the stars in the constellation. Your life has been shaped by your parents, influences, early formative and late, essentially modifying in their thrust, schooling, marriage, your offspring, but there is something a priori encoded in "trailing clouds of glory do we come from God," and "your setting is elsewhere." Reality perhaps, the soul's code is in your Zodiac of which we know nothing about. Perhaps, nobody does including the space scientists. In the absence of this knowledge we have an array of projections by the seers and astrologers of the hoary antiquity and contemporary diviners. These projections have endured for thousands of years unlike human projections which are here today and gone tomorrow. So these projections have taken on the substance of truth and insight.

In KNOW YOUR ZODIAC, I have given psychological spin to the Zodiacs, how they are perceived. In reading the book you do not take everything in my interpretation of a given Zodiac because it would not be applicable in toto. You take whatever seems right and relevant and how and what it triggers in you. The important thing is what you appropriate and what it does for you and how it repercusses. Considered from this angle KNOW YOUR ZODIAC is a heuristic piece, do be kit for use on oneself and one's experiencing of others, of life, situations and scripts. Perhaps, your cardinal personality is clued in your constellation. Personality theorists such as Aldous Huxley, Erich Fromm, Gordon Allport postulate a cardinal/primary personality. You may equate it with the archetypal personality. That part of portion therein which is activated for you. The fact of the matter is that we know precious little about such numinosities. What we know is the personality from parents, nurture, schooling and colleging period and it s modification from the procreative period. Perhaps, the cardinal personality espied in childhood, and later on in periods of difficulty and transition and then in old age when there is nothing much we can do about it is a many-layered aspect of the archetype which is warped for the most part through the secondary and tertiary personalities developed and conditioned, nurtured and cultivated. The cultivated personality should not be at variance with the constellation personality, though the latter too has to be chastened and refined.

One may argue as to why your Zodiac is inordinately important when in one's life, your planets transit through so many Zodiac. Earth spins and comes under the panoply of Zodiacs other than the birth Zodiac. The commonsense answer to this is that the Zodiac at the time of one's birth impresses one with its vibrations. Just as childhood is your matrix, likewise your Zodiac determines the matrix of your root nature, your primordial personality.

ARIES

Natural leader is he
not a politician
because he is straight forward and transparent
Swift is he
and strong
As a tempest, not a wave

Impulses goad him
not transient or processed
or canned emotions

Women who are not impassive
are drawn to him
because he is passionate
and in the admiration mode

When Aries is jealousy-possessed though
he/she becomes querulous, rancorous
the malingering foot-soldier make-believing
that he is a Brigadier
though quilted in the bed, he thinks he is in the cock-pit

Aries is a fire-sign. As such it is naturally compatible with Leo and Sagittarius, but what one needs for balancing, rounding, and augmenting is Aquarius and Gemini. Fire needs air to burn and spread.

Aries is invariably abuzz with projects. Even the relationship is a project for him. He walks away from lukewarm, lackadaisical relationship. Even a three day sudden romance is a project for him.

He is like Johny Applessed, Christ's Sower of seeds. Some seeds fall on the roadside and are eaten by the fowls of the air, some fall into the thorny bushes; some fall into thin soil and are scorched by the sun. Some fall into deep soil yielding return, three-fold, seven-fold, thirty-fold, hundred-fold. Aries moves on with Johny Applessed outlook and he is not looking for admiration or gratitude.

Because of this project orientation it appears to the sentimentalist that he is not emotional when the fact of the matter is that he is passionate and forthright in his emotions. He is an upfront personality, Aries is.

So don't look from him the delicate sensitivity of Virgo, the tangled intensities of Cancer who is into possessiveness, and the balanced equilibrium/ homeostasis of feelings of a Libra. He does not like cold, impassive people who take too much time in warming. He is a man in a hurry to consummate. He cannot go on a prolonged courtship. If that's your need, go to Aquarius. If you need to settle down, build a home and raise a family, go to Cancer. Taurus will do that too for you. Aries is bold and quick on the draw.

Aries are high on instinctive and emotional energy. In routinised living this energy remains on the back-burner. But they need expression of this Bios from time to time to let go, for them to enter into altered states which give them creativity and insight.

Aries can argue for the sake of argument. He must vent his energy. If Aries does not have some one to butt, he will just butt the stump of a tree. In order for Aries to turn his energy into positivity and use it for common weal, it must seek Aquarian people. Gemini people would also help the Arians as Geminis are into mind and imagination. In such relationships Arian energy finds a direction.

Aries has certain problems. He is not able to figure the dark. Dissident, mean and nasty side of people. To his dying day he cannot move away from innocence and integrate into it the dark experiences.

He is impatient. At least he is perceived that way. To frustrate him certain people close to him become cussedly dilatory. Perhaps, he moves from insufficient, inadequate thought to premature action. He is not hungry for result, though. If result comes and matches his expectation, he is happy. But it is does not, he is not going to stop his impulse-goaded activities.

Before I leave Aries, my impressions and cogitations relating to it, it has to be clearly understood that each Zodiac has to be cultured, its positivities have to be augmented and refined; its negativities and problematies have to be clearly identified, encountered, and loosened. The energy inhering in the negativities is tremendous. We need that energy for use to brighten the positivities and also for direct use in certain situations. The relationship between the positivities and negativities is psychodynamic. The polarities have to be harnessed into gestalt, for holistic hermeneutics and dynamic living.

Arians must take to introspection but not to the point where they impair their energy and are sicklied over with a pale cast of thought.

TAURUS

Onyx-eyed
Strong-shouldered
Full-chested Your Taurusis a steady worker
from dawn to dusk
his energy indefatigable –

When dharmic with an active disposition
Rises to sublime heights

Becomes the mount of the gods

Overwork his syndrome
always in harness
collapsing suddenly before the field be ploughed

Because Taurus is a hard worker, he has to be appreciated and fed well. When you come across a house-wife who does not serve a good fare to a hardworking mate and does not offer affirmation, she has herself to blame for the deterioration of the relationship.

A good farmer sees to it that his ox gets proper hay at the end of the day and a few genuine pats. One farmer would close the barn door and feed his ox with oats and wheat grains. In the course of this procedure he would speak to his ox, pat and message, and scrub his thighs. Though innocent of literature, he understood Chekov.

Let us not forget that the bull is a domestic. Without his day in and day out work in the fields, there would be no life. The agrarian age was a quantum jump, a paradigm shift from the hunting age. The ox was the basis of prosperity. No wonder the bull was worshipped. He is still worshipped in India. He is the mount of Shiva.

Taurus' life is sacrifice. Even in his death he is of great use. His hide is used for making shoes.

Soothing and relaxing is the ambience of Cancer for Taurus. To unwind, Taurus can use the beauty and refinement of Cancer. Pisceans with their fluent, unshackled movements and 'negative capability' too offer a change. With them Taureans can defatigue and chill out.

The Ox is flogged while yoked and ploughing the fields. His tail is twisted to give a zap to accelerate him while he is ploughing. But he is patient and forbearing. He takes it as part of his life. He does not show any resentment. You cannot do that to your dog. He will yelp and snarl. If Taurus goes berserk, the whole family is at fault. In such a case family Dynamic Psychology of George Napier and Virginia Satir is needed.

Taurus' problem is contentment. Resultantly, he misses on unusual initiative. He does not take high risks. He thinks that nature is regular. He does not know that nature can be sudden, disruptive and has swift-rushing gods, and those in tune are rewarded with perilous leaps. But Taurus is work-a-coholic, though a steady state worker.

GEMINI

At ease with all signs
Fascinating is Gemini full of surprises
gives them insights drawn from life
from air and ambience

Thought in androgyny near-complete
yet commerces with the mart
has surpluses to sell
ideas to give gratis
or for fee or barter

Beyond the ken of stolid humans
distrusted even by the gods
Nimble wit beams through flux
Outwits categories and freeze-frames
with wings in his feet

Freedom-deprived
clapped in a tree bark
he dies
Liberty the entelechy

He is Energy evolving, revolving, transforming

If Gemini comes under the sway of the malefic
he becomes a low-down trickster
a cheater losing his purpose and élan

If Gemini is the presiding deity of scientists, inventors, journalists, writers he is also the patron of thieves, crooks, and tricksters. He is not professional though. Once he has earned something substantial, he goes legit.

It is useless to tell Geminis to be on their guard. Firstly they are transparent. Secondly, they stick out their neck because they make up things on the run. They believe they can wriggle out of any situation. Reality to them is not factuality, but inventiveness and imagination in which they excel.

Relating is a meta-need with Geminis. He relates across class, caste, creed, country, and religion. Through relationship casual and sustained he gets information, knowledge, and insight. Because of this meta-ability he flows easily, fluently into the intrinsic rhythm of the other. This point should never be lost sight of as it is an egregious folly to think that Geminies are company-hungry.

Gemini's problematic is not realizing that meta-needs cannot be met with in the humdrum life with its wear and tear. Majority of the people are into routine and they are ignorant or innocent of the satisfaction that results from the fulfillment of meta-needs. So Gemini has to reorient himself, look for special, special bonds of a Goldmund for a Narcissus, of Siddhartha for Vasudeva, of Rumi for Shamas Tabrez.

More than only other sign Gemini needs to chill out and to detox because he piles up too much from living. He needs short-term goals to long-term projects for harnessing his surplusages. Gemini, fertile and imaginative is invariably one step ahead of the work in hand. From this he needs alchemically speaking the fellowship of Capricorn and Aquarius.

Aries and Leo can give a local habitation and a name to Gemini's imaginings. Gemini's visions are not grandiose. They are not visitations from the supernal. They stem from hunches, hints, and glowworm glimmering. If in your horoscope Geminis and Aries are well-placed, you have it made. Invoke Gemini where three roads meet or chant to him in a cave.

In Greek mythology Hermes Trismegistus is the Lord Liege of Gemini. He is the son of Zeus and human mother Maia. As a child he fed himself and his mother on tortoise meat. He made a lyre from the tortoise shell, and his first chant was to his mother and absentee father Zeus. He stole sixty heads of cattle from Apollo as a young child and when the case went to Zeus' court, it was dismissed, such was his sophistry. He was made a god and Apollo gave him his staff of authority, and Hermes gave to Apollo his lyre as a return gift.

The motifs in the story are androgyny, cleverness, and divinization.

In one alchemical story he is a river of Mercury. In order to harvest mercury the practitioner situates a pretty girl near its bank. He has troughs dug near the bank. Fascination propelled Mercury lunges again to reach her. Consequently, Mercury is trapped in tubfuls. So Gemini needs the spell of beauty to coagulate.

Gemini can be Icarian and tumble in airy nothing, losing connection with reality. He then is a disembodied gleam unable to disperse darkness. In such a case he will amount to nothing.

CANCER

Blessed by the great Mother who dwells in the Moon
Cancer is the sap of life
Nad's resonance

A home-mother given to esthetics and refinement
simulates much more than what is there
but is not into dissimulation

Buffetted by currents
and hit by lightning
has flashes from within
Underneath the carapace is gooey inside

Because Cancer person is soft and vulnerable because of feeling matrix, in childhood he/she develops a very-near impregnable frontal personality. In due course he/she ceases to be adventurous for which one has to trust and take risks. If this process of defence mechanism goes too far, he/she becomes hermetical. Some Cancerians have a mélange of frontal personalities, which they take on, a bit from here and a bit from there. They embed themselves, becoming part and parcel of their psyches.

Cancerians are not social and outgoing like Gemini, they are not bold like Aries and Saggitarius. They are initially introverted.

Cancerians are essentially family people. They are close to the family of origin, sometimes so close that they do not marry. They like large families. It is a part of their security system. Family is the cardinal reality for them. They may have a lot of discord and disharmony, but they will not opt out.

They like to cut a figure in the eyes of the family. Sometimes they become negative. They become possessive and dominative and don't like any member of the family breaking away from their hold.

Cancer people are not leaders like Aries, Gemini, nor pioneers like Saggitarians as they confine themselves to themselves, their families, and immediate surroundings. The other is seen as an extension of the self or receives the cathexis in the secondary narcissism scheme. It's my servant, my driver, my pet.

Cancer feeling is deep, but confined. Its focus is strong, but narrow and exclusionary. Not for the Cancerian to go for constellatory psychology. If the Cancerian is into guru, he cannot accept other gurus.

Cancer people are content for the most part with their boundary walls and flower pots, content with their rise to middle-rung positions. Not for them the transformation mysteries unless they get a hit from the moon or the lightning. They are clingers who won't let go with their hold-fast syndromes. They should look for Jupiterian people with learning and spirituality to grow and go places. And they usually do.

Cancerians often have a very passionate life. They love their children but sometimes their passionate life can be at the expense of their children. This problem surfaces in the early years of marriage.

Cancerians are not ambitious. Family and home give them contentment, not achievement in the world out there.

LEO

Perhaps, the most ambitious
materialistic-to-the extreme sign
and spiritual in enantiodromia like king Ashoka
Feeling is lazer sharp
Hearing predatory acute

He has to work to a code with vigour
otherwise he becomes lapsed, tamsic soul
a lazy bum looking for destiny
for apple pie in the sky

No sickness is comparable to Leo's sickness,
You become a dope-head, an absinthe-drinker

skidrow drop-out
who make believes that he is curdling
space with roars of awakening

Leo must aggrandize
to justify itself

Unless purpose comes into his life, there is no redemption. Without purpose he is appetitive, aggressive, a parasite. Gemini with his motility can give him a direction. He should allow Libra to give him a sense of equity and justice. But Leos do not surrender as they think no end of themselves. They carry a sense of superiority. Feeling culture is dismal. They have to be UNO Numero.

They are the poorest in maintaining relationships. They shoo away people with their aggression which stems from their pride. The question of mending broken relationship does not arise because they are incapable of seeing their role in the breakage and consequently incapable of feeling-remorse.

If Leo embraces a line of work genuinely, he will excel in it, for he is a perfectionist, but he has to not use his putative excellence to bolster his superiority- his Achilles heel.

As a young man Leo is into thinking, in the thickening forties into feeling; in the sixties into bio-energetics. Phooey

Leos are very particular about their territory and privacy, but they do not extend that courtesy to others. They intrude into space which does not belong to them. They poach and aggrandize.

They do not fee self-conscious about ferreting your secrets, but are very guarded about themselves. They are cunning and calculating.

They want power, but when unable to secure it they develop paranoia. In Buddhist terminology they are titans. Now every Leo can not become a titan, so majority settle for being dwarf titans, more dwarfs than titans, dwarfs with Pisach orientation.

In the foregoing pages, for good and bad, I have dealt with the pathology of the Leos, but it was also stated that if the Leo comes to purpose, he is unstoppable. And if he accepts the reverence and guru principle in an existential way in the sense of looking up to elders, father figures, he embarks from purpose to destiny. With the acceptance of guardians he becomes a guardian himself protecting the people and coming through for all and sundry. If Leo has a relationship with Aquarius in the chart, he becomes dynamised. I once met a surgeon in a reputed Hospital who had this combination and he had gone places. The surgeon radiated force professionally and exuded grace.

Leo on cusp close to Virgo is very positive. Then he has Virgo's sensitivity and delicacy, but Leo's forwardness and strength.

Leos are enormously talented. Leo can come into his potency and power only through a woman. It is interesting to note that in the Tarot cards Leo is depicted as a leonine-faced royal figure carrying a nude, Venusian woman in his arms. It is a very Blakean picture.

VIRGO

Tender, sensitive
Coy, not given to emoting
not being upfront
emotion deep, but recessive

When Virgo falls into dissipation
for whatever reason
declension is non-stop
becomes he a cockroach in the garbage pail

She a chickey-poo who is wailing
in the chipped kitchen-sink

Virgo are not into people like Geminis nor like Aquarians extending themselves to help people. They do not have extroverted élan and span. Because they are introverted, they are misunderstood as being cold. In their relational script they are into their families and a few friends. Virgos can never make it big. They do not have overvaulting ambition. Not for them to follow Faustus because they have innate scruples and instinctive values stemming from the archetype of the Feminine. When Virgo departs from the archetype, he ruins himself and others. Round and round in the ruinous circles he spins, diffusing stench, some through catharsis, some through repetitive-compulsive besotted sexuality. In such eventualities he must know procedures of sublimation like taking to a project in which they can take pleasure, to keep the depression at bay and imbuing their life with meaning; worshipping the Divini Mother, assuming anima-rich female nature. It is not sadhana. Easy does it because it is both rewarding and enjoyable.

The greatest problem for Virgos is purity resulting from repression. They become parodic fauns gamboling on antic hay or puritanical prigs wanting to castrate nuts...

Pleasure without purpose is sterile. Purpose without pleasure is robotic.

Virgos are gentle and sensitive, delicate withal. They are fragile. Their sign Virgin has nothing to do with Kali and Durga, but with Mother Mary who is the mother of seven sorrows. When a Virgo woman gets angry, she has no control. It shakes her nerve strings. Hysteria is not good for Virgos.

Virgos are in the romantic mood. They should not marry rough, tough Zodiac like Leo, practical, materialistic Zodiac like Capricorns, erratic, elective Zodiac like scorpion.

Once I came across two Virgos. They were twins who shared the navel, but their lives were so different. One was simple, organized, spoke little, but was a good husband and a good provider; his elder twin brother drifted from small-time business to small-time jobs, had no direction, borrowed, spoke too much. One comes across such radical opposites in this sign.

LIBRA

Is the rain-maker
no civilization, culture evolves
without her,
She balances claims and counter-claims
completing clamorous interests
in the balancing scales of justice-

Is into rational consciousness tempered
with the categorical imperative of justice

Is into beauty and harmony
is king and compassionate

With her the decisive entry into ethics
though existential is she
with sorge for the other

Ideas alienate you from feelings which stem from a rich, resonant conscience. It is not that Libra does not think, but it sub-serves feeling. Gandhi and Churchill are prime examples of Libra. They are into dialectics and transcendence which contains the thesis and anti-thesis in the new gestalt.

Librans are sensitive to spiritual susceptibilities. Since they are into order and esthetics, the leap into spirituality is easy. Their spirituality is existential, not in the theological sense, but naturally. They sense the numinous in dream and wake, into relationship and unhesitatingly go with it.

Saturn is perhaps the greatest thinker among the planets, transpersonal in its location, reach, and sweep. In Indian astrology unfortunately he is demonized for the most part. He is exalted in Libra where he is harmonized in a home where custom is the laurel tree and ceremony the horn of plenty.

Librans are kind and considerate. Not for them to wish ill to anybody. There is no malice in them, and they are not personally retributive. For them punishing the guilty and iniquitous is the right of the gods.

Librans are sattvic in their ahaar. They avoid alcohol and are into nutritious non-stimulating diet. Unlike Scorpions who can crunch fist and flesh and drink a great deal, Librans are teetotalers. Their sense of taste is simple, but delicate. They are not into strong spicing.

They are judicial and judicious in their relationship. Fair dealing comes naturally to them.

Librans may be affluent, but they are not into money-making as such. They regard contentment as their wealth, and they are generous whenever and wherever they can. Some Librans excel in anonymous donations.

Librans are not appetitive sexually, though they like an aesthetic love life based on sharing and doing things together. Like Cancer they have a strong sense of the family, but are not possessive and appropriative like Cancer.

They are very good hosts and welcome relatives and friends dropping in and sharing their meal with them. They are into fasting too which is their way of purifying their system and connecting with the divine. They need the numinous. Everybody does as a matter of fact, but they work at it by visiting temples, churches, synagogues, monasteries. Usually they have friends in spiritual circles who are affectionate with them.

Usually they are happy in their married life because they do not cheat. Secondly, they are into adjusting and understanding the partner's point of view and are into harmony. They do not enjoy quarrels and fights. They harmonize easily with Aries, Taurus, Saggitarious, and Aquarius. Leos, Virgos, Capricorns, Pisceans, Cancers are not compatible with them though Librans with their innate sense of mutualism and harmony can get along with them without ripples and ruckus.

Librans run to a pattern. Their Ahara is pure, they are just and ethical in their conduct.

SCORPIO

With fire in the tail
loves cool places
Explores inner spaces
is into the unseen and solitude
and how it impinges the visible
he is your mystic in the Zodiac round

Magmas explode from within
of sublimity and pathology

You'll come across the finest specimens
of mystics and titans
but also twisted somnambules
who hunt at nigh

Scorpio is perhaps the most difficult sign sandwiched between two straightforward Zodiacs, Libra and Saggitarius.

Scorpios have very sharp reactions in regard to situations and people. They are concerned with conduct, codes, and values and they react to lapses. Like Libra people they are sensitive to spiritual susceptibilities. Apart from personal growth and efflorescence of potentials and numens resulting from spiritual commitment, spirituality enables them to handle their reactivity which cannot be wished away.

Scorpios carry resentment over a period of time. Here they are different from Aries who express it, are upfront and let it out through abuses and curses. Aries expressive strategy obliterates resentment. There is no setting of Scores. Scorpios may not settle scores, but they inwardly write off bounders. Outwardly they may not show it, may every interact with them because of family, social norms and cultural concerns, but bounders do not constitute even a footnote in their book.

Scorpios, by and large, have great regard for cultural values and norms. It is good to take advice from them. Scorpio is occult. It has the power to bless and curse. Evolved Scorpios bless naturally and enthusiastically. They do not curse. But their hurt hits the bad guys. It is part of discretion and intelligence to avoid inflicting hurt on the Scorpios.

A family of three brothers came to a Scorpio for advice regarding division of assets after their father's demise.

One brother had the ancestral, one had the shop, the third had built his own house through hard work and saving. He had retired as Professor of Commerce in a Delhi College.

The Scorpio guide advised "In your Bania community you would spilt even the father's cane in three parts. In any division women get involved. Relations are spoiled. Let the brother living in the ancestral house keep it, the shopkeeper keep the shop. The professor the eldest who has brought you up is not covetous. The family gold should be given to the three sisters equally."

The matter was settled in ten minutes. Perhaps, it should be pointed out that Scropios make excellent therapists. They maintain confidentiality, pace the catharsis, elucidate problems and potentials with superior understanding, and give a value base for personality reconstitution.

Scorpios are very hard workers. They plan their work, structure and pace, excel in mastering the myriad details and how they fit the overall blue print. They don't rush in cartographing the blue print, but once prepared, they implement it with a thoroughness and finesse.

Because of planning, structuring, commitment, from humble beginnings they rise and scale commanding heights.

If Shiva has Vasuki around his neck, vipers around his wrists, cobras guarding the crescent moon in his head, his matted locks are full of Scorpions. Scorpions should worship the Divine Mother as they are Shivaganas.

Scorpios are difficult customers. If you think you are close to them and you can make them do something simple like reading a manuscript, you are mistaken. If Scorpio thinks that you are putting pressure on him, his tail is up. It is advisable for you to retreat. Scorpios are not helpful, when pressured.

It is difficult to figure out scorpios because they are not upfront. It is difficult to figure out what they are thinking and feeling. If you think you are bigger in position, status, influence, you can humiliate him, you are mistaken. He will unhorse you and turn you into mush.

SAGITTARIUS

Is a visionary
shoots arrows in space
bringing down the constellations

The given, the factitious bores you
You are at the cutting edge of thought
and technology

Sagittarius sturdy stalwart swallowing
distances

Farther, farther sail
Follow knowledge like a sinking star
beyond the utmost bound of human thought

Dangerous is Sagittarius
without reality check
without anchorage in Antaeus
with feet on the ground

Makes you perish in a swamp
with Will o' wisp with migraine in the head
with bhekel thorn piercing the flesh
Sagittarius go to Libra
for harmony
to Aquarius for service-
Reconcile vision and fact

Sagittarius are full of ideas, actual, practical, symbolic, imaginal which they actualize because of bios on one hand and enthusiasm on the other. His bios comes from being horse up to the neck, and enthusiasm from the half man with powerful shoulders shooting a volley of arrows into the firmament.

Unfortunately nine out of ten Saggitarians have pipe dreams and vacuous wings. They are surly titans beating their wings in the void. The Old Man Santiago in Hemingway's Old Man and the Sea prepares for eighty days before launching out into the deep sea. He prepares himself by eating turtle eggs by the kilos.

Sagittarius develop their script down to earth and soaring high early in life. The script has to be clarified progressively.

On the positive side Saggitarious is optimistic, versatile, sincere, visionary, open-minded, philosophical, frank, and Jovial.

On the downside he is tactless, careless, irresponsible, lazy, wasteful, restless when not able to balance the theriomorph with the human, and two turned to aspiring or the celestial....

CAPRICORN

Thinks that everything can be enveloped
through reason and criticality
Organises life with schedules
society with rules
is into conventional consciousness
through which he controls the composite
subliminal

but the control slips. The eruptions give mood-swings
In due course criticality vis-à-vis others is introspected vis-à-vis oneself too.

Capricorn can carry grudges over a long span of time. Can carry into his next life.

Though a ritualist, he is indiscriminate and various in appetites. Because Capricorn arranges his identity around reason and criticality, he needs, Pisces perhaps for loosening the hard knot of his identity. He can also turn to Scorpio for mysticality and occult for self-charging.

Capricorns are more organized than Virgos. Resultantly they can keep many projects going at the same time. They are practical and are not into Arian flights nor into space probes scavenging the skies. If Capricorn is on cusp looking back to Saggitarius or looking forward to Aquarius, he gets the tincture of their positive qualities. Cusp leads to enrichment and beneficial augmentation.

Despite what has been said above regarding Capricorn's skill in tossing many balls in the air like a magician and not letting any fall on the ground, it should also be borne in mind that on the downside slippage path they move from project to project without bringing any to fruition. It should also be further outlined that his projects subserve his narcissism. They are devoid of idealism. They have no depth or sweep. And they don't have relevance for the polity. So beware of Capricorns when they want to do something for you. They mean well. They will initiate preliminary steps in that direction, but because of lack of perseverance and poor follow-up their intentions perish in the sand.

Capricorns lack the capacity to admire. The shadow of criticality and judgement erodes their admiration. The worst aspect of the Capricorns is that they mock their elders and teachers who have done a great deal for them.

In contrast Gemini's projects are for pleasure, for sheer delight. Cancer's projects usually are around the house pertaining to family and friends. Cancerians excel in interiors where he seeks beauty. There is no impulse and spontaneity to Capricorn's projects. For projects as natural eruptions you have to go to Aries. Capricorn's projects are deliberate. They are carefully crafted. The motive is self-projection and self-advancement, their relational script being poor and at best transactional.

Unlike Aries whose decisions come from the impulse centres and their won evaluation, Capricorn goes for wide consultancy. If they want to buy a one-room flat in a hill station to enable their family to vacation for a week or so, he would go over it taking inputs from friends, property dealers, family members, and even astrologers.

However, once the die is cast over a venture, Capricorn works very hard to pull it off and get it going. Here they are different form Pisceans who take too long a time to come to closure. Sometimes their closure is an escape from vacillation and restlessness, and they work at the project with tremendous insight and energy though fitfully. Pisceans cannot settle for something which jut brings bread and bacon. They are grandiose dreamers.

Capricorn is into himself. His narcissism extends, and embraces the family. Beyond the dialectic love stops. Psychologically they seldom go beyond secondary narcissism which may include in addition to one's family a few friends.

Since Saturn is the Lord of Capricorn, you may come across Capricornians who are into the transpersonal. In such cases their transpersonality disconnects them from the mundane, from reality. It is fine for them to aspire to the transpersonal, but the homework involved is to bring the higher thinking and superfine energy down to inform life and suffuse relations. The quotidian and the transcendent must come together. The resistances from the mundane have to be thinned through and surrender to the power of the higher entelechies.

AQUARIUS

Is a pre-eminent sigh of service and other orientation, one has to see though that philanthropy does not become egotistical sublime. Because people are narcissitic they cannot understand a good Samaritan. They look for motives. "There must be something in it for him," argue the skeptics. But for Aquarius to help is his natural impulse. In order for Aquarius to help beneficently and effectively Aquarians must develop insight and skill. And even when he has acquired a fund of insight and skill, he has to see that he cannot be too sure. Inside he should feel somewhat anxious and not too certain. An Aquarian may be extraordinary in insight, skill, but he has to reckon with the fact that those receiving help usually do not make a requisite opening. Majority take a bid and bumble on, not realizing that the course is not complete. Ego alongwith distrust comes in the way. We blame the helpless. So Aquarians unfortunately take a lot of abuse.

But good Aquarians like George Washington subject to doubt and vacillation despite experience and confidence understand that life is a die game, and that choose one must.

You are choosing for others for whom you are responsible. The above should not be taken to mean that Aquarian does not have problems, but that does not mean that he should quit helping out. Helping others will enable him to help himself in due course. I remember telling a holy man, "People turn to me with all kinds of problems. I respond, but feel weird because I have insurmountable problems." The holy man replied, "Respond. Input. Solving problems of others will help you to solve your own too."

I am not an Aquarian, but the advice of the Holy man is especially relevant for Aquarians.

Your Aquarian is a gifted healer
tall and handsome
with a scintillating skin

You can call him at midnight
And he is there at your doorstep
to help you out
to bail you out of calamity

If he has the wherewithal
he parts with macro millions

PISCES

Pisces is perhaps the most difficult sign because it is mediumistic. If Gemini can become the other through mind and imagination, Piscean does so without realizing through the leap of feeling and intuition. It takes on the personalities of other Zodiacs and loses itself in the labyrinthine round. The homework involved is having some semblance of one's own identity without losing one's empathy which is the source of intuition and knowledge accruing therefrom. Pisces, however, is not supposed to take on the identity of other Zodiacs except fluently, taking and leaving and returning to its own reality. Unfortunately they get trapped in certain identifications. Because Pisces can moo like a moose and roar like a lion, so on and so forth, it is difficult for others to comprehend it, and Pisces' identifications are difficult to decipher.

Pisceans need the influence of Taurus to make a commitment to work and that of Capricorn to cultivate a sense of criticality and a sense of reality.

When Pisceans withdraw from life, from aquamarine of feeling and become secretive, they shrivel and become denizens of shallow backwaters. Growth stops. They take to carping and whining. Pisceans should not rage either, their natural element is feeling fluency and intuitive at-one-ment with the seethe of life fluxing, circumambient around them. If Piscean gets a benefactor, it goes far. From a small foil it becomes a whale, but for that to happen, Pisceans have to have sight and clarity in discrimination. One is reminded in this context of Manu's fist. Manu, the Indian progenitor of an eon and the law giver who reciting the Gayatri standing in river water waist deep caught a small fist in his round worship copper vessel. When he was about to throw the tiny fish back into the waters, the fish wailed "I am so tiny. I'll be eaten by other creatures in the water." Manu brought the tiny fist home; he kept her in a jar of water in his meditation room. In course of time the fish became too big for its small container. Manu put her in his backyard pond where he used to grow lotuses for his worship. The fish grew to enormous size in a year's time; it would lay stock-still from one end of the pond to the other end. It appeared to Manu that it must be weighing 1500 pounds. When Manu was thinking what he should do now, the fish spoke "You have taken care of me with tender, loving care. Now you can take me back to Sutlej." But how," Manu asked, stumped. A few days later Manu drafted the entire village to build an oak frame from logs. The fish was carted. Once in the Sutlej she just sailed down like a Yacht and disappeared from sight in the twinkling of an eye." Manu said to the wonder-struck villagers "My daughter would soon be in the Arabian sea." Years later when Sutlej flooded and was about to inundate Manali, Manu's fish appeared and hoisted the village folks together with Manu on her back and towed them to safety.

Though spiritual, Pisceans sometimes become grossly materialistic because of a sense of acute deprivation, real, fanciful or imaginal. In such cases they fall into pathology. J.D. Salinger has written a story in which a banana fish has gobbled so many bananas that it sinks and drowns in the bottom of the sea.

So it is important for Pisceans to develop their psychic faculties and spiritual susceptibilities. They have to follow Peter who left fishing to follow Christ and became a great fisher of men.

Though every constellation has a problematic side, Piscean's problematic side has to be now problematised. Being mediumistic they have to stay in the psychic and spiritual locale. If they don't do that, they will be untrue to themselves. Once in authenticity sets in, it would be difficult to retrieve oneself. No other sign is as restless. She is tossing in the waters of *vrittis*. Piscean has to learn to stay stock-still to discover her personhood, an identity stemming therefrom. A medium has a dream in which she looks at herself in the mirror. She finds that she has no head. She is petrified in the dream. The fact of the matter is that a medium too has a head, an identity. Even a sufi who has experienced Fana has a leshmatra personality which is not to be devalued. It may be that of a scholar, poet, a musician, an interior decorator. It is essential for the medium to cultivate that phantom personality and have a mediumistic relationship with it to help it grow and effloresce. The homework for Pisceans is elaborate.

1. To secure their feeling function, chastening and purifying it for the intuition to move through the crystal glass.
2. To develop an expanse and depth to feeling. Feeling is water whereas sensation is earth, thinking air, and intuition fire. Unfortunately majority of the Pisceans swim in dirty ponds of their own devising.

Pisceans usually are gifted linguistically, they experience nano states and if they are blessed with memory, they can regale the listeners with sequences and serials and take to extraordinary sensitive writing. They can make very good face readers, fortune tellers, and artists.

Pisceans should never be into power. It does not come to

them naturally. In pursuit of power they are swimming against their grain. Pursuit of power is debilitating for the most part.

Pisceans being mediumistic should not follow. When a Piscean becomes a follower, he/she invites a double injury- one to her gift and second to her residual identity. She is not in the business of giving a sales pitch for any leader. Aries, Geminis, Leos, Libras, Sagittarius, Scorpios are leaders in varying ways, some through excess of adrenalin, communication, some through violence, vision, love of justice. Piscean way is neither leading nor following. It is seeing that you see.

Pisceans are seers
They see today
see what will unfold in the next century

Their seeing fabular
not mimetic
It has to be rendered through images
and symbols
Hasidic their use of language

True Pisceans should avoid becoming
face-readers, fortune-tellers, horoscope
chariatans

Ensconced in the cave under water
they can transmit their hieroglyph
to superior men
for human kind to use

It is painful to see them writhe though
in the net of Maya
They can swim through its holes
and be free
But alas!

In the practicum of living
they go back and forth
such flickering flip-flops
they exhaust spouse, offspring, Amor
friend
with their postponement
vacillation no end

They see not
that vision has to be handed over
to deed, swift, straight, and frank
to aesthesis
to the faculties, executive

Precisely because of triune lack
they nostalagise
on what could have been

But it does not have to be that way
Pisceans are enormously talented
They can be actors, enter-tainers,
to-what-you-will folks, who wax
in the stream of becoming and experience
and become benefactors and saviours

Pisces's principal problem is that they are pulled in opposite directions. The fault is not in the waves or circumstances and others around them, but of the divisiveness in them. To get a grip on themselves, their wasting themselves and not amounting too much, they should invoke Brihaspati who missed being a second sun. They should accept the guidance of the elders. To speak precisely, they should accept the careers/exemplars of the archetype of the Wise Old Man.

Part II

An astrologer friend of mine who had become my guide when I took to studying with him sent me the following personal note in the emotive vein which I am sharing with you, my reader.

My dear Aziz,

You asked me to make a personal emotive statement in regard to the constellations to serve as an appendix to your little book. So here it goes without preliminaries in the first person singular. I feel comfortable with Ares. They are upfront and forthright. They can be trusted as friends. And as enemies too. So one is safe. Besides, if Ares is your enemy to-day, he can be your friend tomorrow. He is not rancorous. He is energy; his intelligence, sensibility is an expression thereof.

I feel very comfortable with Taurus too. His energy is high, but domesticated. He is a hand-working provider and is always working his butt off. But in my practice I have found that most families do not appreciate his hard work which is taken for granted. Even in death he leaves his parts and limbs for the family to partake of. We should be grateful to Taurians. They hold the earth on their horns. In Greek mythology they are Atlases. They suffer from colic, from Bursitis. In my language they are a commix of physico-vital or vital physical, pure in heart, but where the synastry is bad because the wife expects, in addition to work and service, frills and extended romantic holidays, he goes berserk. I once had to read the awfully ugly relationship between a Taurus and Virgo replete in dysfunctionality and violence.

I like Gemini a whole lot. He is a sparkle and scintillation. Your section on Gemini is excellent, I like the two stories, one Greek, the other from Alchemy. Gemini is known for the motifs of coniunctio and androgyny, brilliant maneuvering, and rich

Devi-tatva or what is called the anima in Western psychology. Hermes, the ruler of Gemini is presented as a figure, half light and half dark, holding a caduceus staff with a dog and a snake, his theriormophs.

Coming from Gemini to Cancer is a let down. Gemini is the Lord of the air while cancer scuttles on a few acres of water on ragged claws. When I read the disposition of cancer in a horoscope in relationship to other Zodiacs and planets, I try to see if Cancer has been hit by lightning and has lost its carapace to the strike. With the hit cancer has to sink or swim.

Cancer has to empower itself socially. I remember a U.S. Couple. The man was a Professor. At the parties which were in vogue in the sixties, she never showed up alongwith him. She was Cancerian. Once in a while I saw him at the parties with the Japanese co-ed, an exchange student boarding with them.

I agree with your brief profile on Leo, though Leos can become powerful sheep dogs if they were to take to Dharma and guardianship. More than any other constellation Leos have to undergo the rite of transformation. But before the rite of rites, they have to go through series of reconstitutions. I have problems with Virgo. It is a high, high sign, sign of Madonna, of the nun and the spiritual mother. Virgos must cultivate a spiritual register and follow the deities and the messengers. They must cultivate their fragile light and illume the world in their shy ways.

You are right with Libra. I don't have anything to add. Their sense of justice is Jupiterian, in beauty they are Venusians. If they stray here and there, it does not matter because in-built in them is mechanism of correction and self-regulation.

Scropio is chthonic and occult. Paranormal powers are common to them. They must link up with the Divine.

You are right about Capricorn. They contribute to material advancement. It is an Artha sign. Capricornian's must turn to

Dharma. Without it they become selfish, capricious, and indiscriminate in their appetites like goats.

Saggitarians can move too fast with their utopian visions. They have to realize that the implementation of visions is within the frame of Desh-kala-Nimit, milieu, moment, and people and instruments conductive to their realization. Without this orientation shadow falls between the vision and reality.

I have nothing to add to or subtract from your profile of Aquarius. But regarding Pisces I must say that out of millions, a few are called and elected to the high destiny of psychic spirituality. A high Piscean can initiate you with a look like Raman Maharishi. Unfortunately though there is a Piscean who becomes a sucker who cleans the teeth of a shark and gets its meat pickings from the gaps in the teeth. No dearth of Pisceans who confine themselves to shallow pools near the banks. One in a million becomes Moby Dick.

Pisces is the sign of the great Mother who puts you through Death and Rebirth.

Good luck on your Zodiac venture. You have the theory right. Rest is practice.

Your friend-

P.S. (1) : I came back to Gemini. You can see my fondness for Geminis. With their imaginative wing-power they are space swallowers, and if they take to systems, they will have a dozen of them inside to order knowledge and experience. "Do I contradict myself/ yes, I do/ I am large, I contain multitudes" is so true of Geminis.

P.S. (2) : It seems to me that you are somewhat unfair to the Pisceans. Pisceans indeed are Hamlets. They do a lot of back and forth. They are not Leos. But something has to be said in favour of this back and forth. One arrives at a better closure. One can take in many points of view and perspectives. One Piscean used to say that he has to do research in the subject before deciding. Pisces however, is the most versatile sign. Pisceans can do anything from business to writing, from acting to politicking-

Part III

PRAXIS

How to use the Zodiacs is the concern of this section. Zodiac is a worthy subject for meditation. Sitting in meditation like one does in any meditation procedure, first visualize space. If you cannot do it, just feel it.

Second, with the help of thought/imagination experience activation, a throb in space allow it to become the constellation.

Thereafter see it throbbing, palpitating its cluster of lights above your head; stay in that attitude as long as you can.

Fourth feel the light/ lights inside at the midpoint between conscious and unconscious. If activation takes place, stay with it.

Fifth, moving to the conscious but retaining the rich connection with the midpoint, introject the Zodiac profile for it to give you knowledge and insight into yourself and others.

In the second procedure centre the corresponding planet in the constellation.

What is being pointed out is not that original. In India lots of people worship the planets for placation, propitiation, and identification. The only difference in this procedure is that it finally aims at dialoging for individuation through relating to a galaxy.

It appears to the author that the ancient seers received the knowledge of the constellations and the planets through meditation procedures which culminated in contemplation and communion. So we are doing in a laboured way what they did naturally, when mythic seeing was a fact, and not an anomaly that it has become in our age of logic and ratiocination.

The seers did not see the goat, the ram, the bull, the crab the scorpion, the fish in the constellations. They experienced their nature and vibrations and in order to facilitate the understanding and relationship of the common man with them they gave the emblems as a code language. It is not possible to experience any Zodiac directly, even a smidgeon, but indirectly through the signs you may connect with your reality.

Different cultures in their mythology have given us information on the signs. The more we connect with the information, with the lore and the stories, better will be our understanding of the Zodiacs. Take for example the scorpion. In Egyptian mythology which is older than Greek mythology Scropions are associated with Isis, the Queen of queens. They protect Isis who is followed by a train of them, and if any one is lacking in deference and harbours ill-will, they sting him to death. So scorpion is a metonymic sign of the great mother.

So Scorpio is a power sign. The power can be spiritual, occult, worldly or a mix of the three.

While we are on the signs, perhaps, it should be pointed out that the sign reader must develop an active imagination especially in the animal signs, in particular. Ram, bull, goat, lion are easy to grasp and scorpion and Pisces. I am somewhat difficult. In reading them one has to be cautious and thorough. The Lady with the scales, with the pitcher of water are straight-forward and easily signs. Virgo is somewhat ambiguous. She is Diana who turns Acteon into a stag and has him torn by her dogs. She is also the Virgin Madonna, the Mother of Christ. She is the Mother of Seven Sorrows.

Saggitarius is again difficult. Any sign which is part animal, part human is challenging.

Pisces does not have the killer instinct. Just as well. The killer instinct has to be replaced by Wu-Wei stance. They should swim with the current cashing it wherever it is possible. This is in line with their mediumistic personality.

CHAPTER 5

The Twelve Houses (Bhavas)

HARISH K THAKUR

The explanation of the charts primarily relies on the structure of a chart which consists of twelve houses, also known as *Bhavan*, *Sthan* or *Bhava*. The counting of the houses is done anti-clockwise, though, the astrologers of South India would differ as they go for the opposite. Each house signifies some specific subjects relating to the chart of the person and consequently their nomenclature also follows the suit.

There are some important things about the Houses which need to be discussed here. Firstly, all the houses of a chart have their natural benefactors. Hence, when we go for the interpretation of the chart this fact requires to be kept in mind.

Secondly, the owner of the sign which has been assigned to a particular house is known as *Bhavesh*. For instance if the sign of Libra is assigned to first house, the owner of the sign Libra i.e. Venus would represent the first house and the things related with the said house such as self, complexion, personality and health etc.

Thirdly, the planet placed in a particular house is the factual owner of the house. For example if Sun is placed in the tenth house it would be known as *Dasmasth* , hence the instant activator of the house.

If in a chart the house number one is occupied by Libra whose owner is Venus and the planet placed is Jupiter, the instant activator. Any prediction of the house, therefore, would have to take into consideration the role of Sun (natural benefactor), Venus and Jupiter, the trio engaged in the house.

Now if we take all the three points we come to know about a complex whole that astrology is. For example we want to observe the house number ten of a chart i.e. the matters related with profession, career, father etc. Here we have to take into consideration the planet placed in the tenth house, i.e. *Dasmasth* which can be more than one, the owner of the sign assigned to the house and the natural benefactor of the house.

Besides this the aspects of the planets over the houses are equally important. The role of a well placed planet is debilitated by the aspects of malefic planets and this need to be studied seriously before passing out a final judgment about the chart. The following chart shows the natural benefactors of a house which means if any of these benefactor is actually placed in that house would bring more success and fruit to it.

The first, fourth, seventh and tenth houses of a chart are also called square or Kendra Bhavas ; second, fifth, eighth and eleventh as Panfar; third , sixth, ninth and twelfth as Apoklim; first, fifth and ninth as Triangle and third, sixth and twelfth as Trika Bhavas.

First House

This house is also known as *Lagna, Tanu, Kalpa, Uday, Vapu or Murti* etc. Since this is the first house it represents the birth, complexion, body structure, face, head, health, disease, nature, character, age, vision, sufferings and happiness of a person.

Normally, the owner of the sign (Lagnesh) of the first house together with the planet or planets placed here (Lagnastha) determine the nature, complexion and other characteristics of a person. If there is no planet placed in the first house then the owner of the sign would be chief consideration while interpreting the house.

All the major things about a person i.e his health, nature, age, profession, happiness, fortunes etc. require to be explored with the position of the Lagnesh and Lagnastha planets.

Sun is the natural benefactor of the first house.

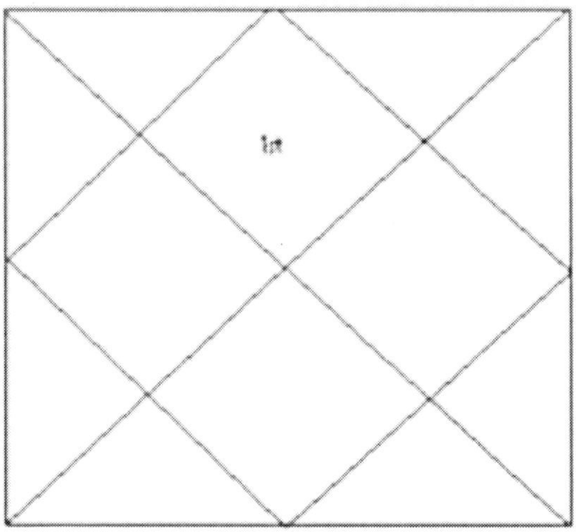

Second House

The second house is also known as Swa, Vaak, Nayan, *Dhana, Marak* or Kutumb bhava.

It represents the family, ancestry, voice, right eye, ear, nose, cosmetics, gems, stone, imagination, memory, scholarship, habits, wealth, bank balance, mouth, speech, elder brother of mother, and larger happiness of the family.

This means all the worldly pleasures that a person can enjoy are reflected by this house since it shows position of his family and the financial condition of a person also. However, there are many other factors which are considered to predict this.

This house has also one notoriety of being *Marak* bhava too i.e. the house of killer planet. The owner of the sign of this house is known as killer or Markesh which becomes more hostile if placed in seventh house which in turn is twelfth in number from the house of death i.e. eighth house. The reason behind the consideration of this house as *Marak* bhava is the fact that it falls twelfth (house of expenditure) from third house, which is eighth when counted from eighth house (house of death).

Jupiter is the natural benefactor of the house.

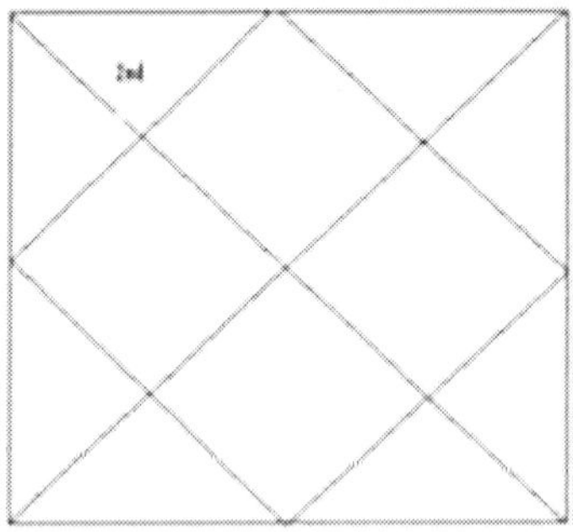

Third House

This house is also known as house of *Valour, Prakram,Veerya, Dhairya and Sahodar* .

This house represents arms, valour, determination, writing, correspondence, reporting, and signature. Younger brothers and sisters and their happiness is also considered from this house. Besides this friends, neighbours, lungs, asthma, cough, respiratory problems, labour and small travels are also represented by this house.

Diseases related with throat infections, respiratory problems, lungs and hands and arms are considered from third house. Mars is the natural benefic of the house.

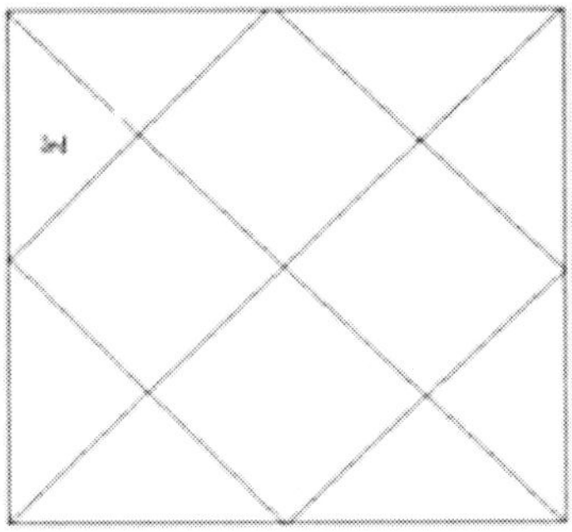

Fourth House

This house is known as *Sukha ,Patal, Matra, Jal,or Bhava of wisdom.*

From this house things of consideration are happiness of life, house, mother, land, property, vehicle, wealth, wisdom, benevolence, adoption, public, and friends. It also represents, land, agriculture, pond, well, cemetery, grandmother (maternal) and father-in-law. Diseases of chest, heart, ribs, stomach and mental illness are also studied from this house. Moon, Venus and Mercury are the natural benefactors of this house.

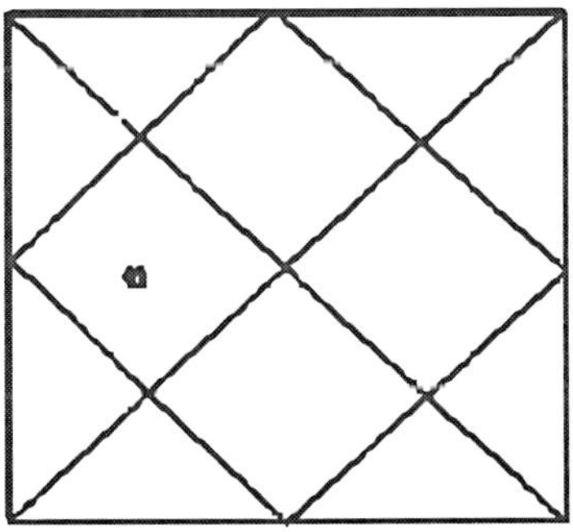

Fifth House

This house is also known as *Sut, Dhee, Nandan, Trikon, Dev and Santaan Bhava.*

From this house education, intelligence, children, love, romance, conception, age of father, husband of elder sister, examinations, disposition, entertainment, sports, horse race, art, dance , singing, digestion, lottery, investment, spiritual knowledge, policy, dialogue etc. are observed.

This house represents the diseases of stomach, liver and kidneys. Jupiter is the natural benefactor of this house.

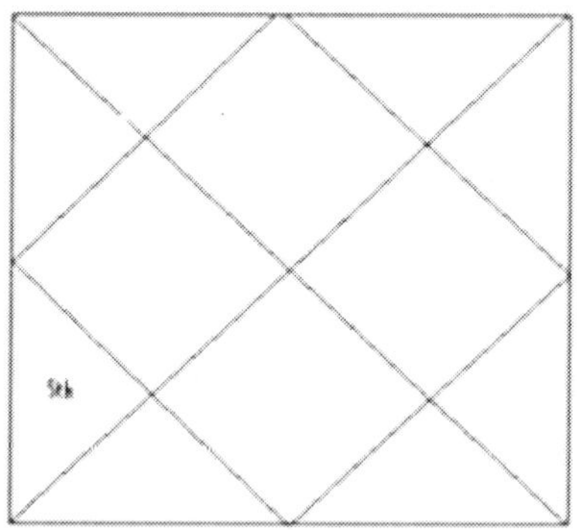

Sixth House

This house is again called by different names such as *Ripu, Trika Bhava or Rog Bhava.*

The subjects like maternal uncle, maternal aunt, diseases, enemies, fear, bankruptsy, suffering, prosecution, quarrels, arrest, tension, boils, injuries, hurdles, intestines, fortunes of father, wealth of sons, enemies of wife or partner, theft, eye problems and lower abdominal diseases are studied from this house.

Since this is Roga Bhava too its owners are considered mostly bad in effect. Appendicitis, waist problems, intestines, hernia etc. are observed from this house. Mars and Saturn are the benefactors of the house.

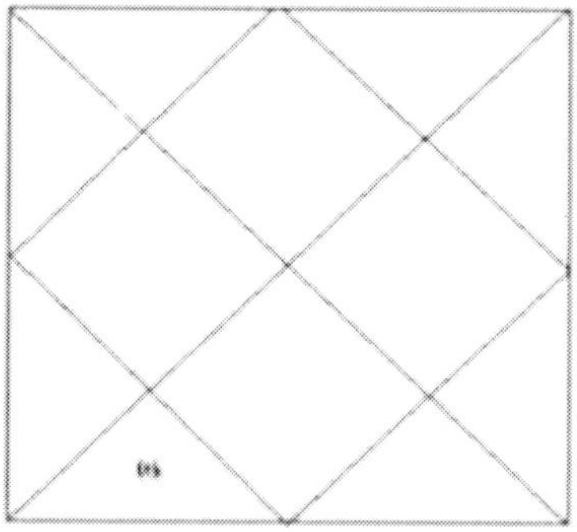

Seventh House

Known by the names of Kaam, Kalatra, Gaman, Sampat, Jamitra, Ast and Marak seventh house primarily represents partners in life.

From the seventh house we study wife, friends, partners, partnerships, trade, commerce, quarrels, competition, happiness of marital life, success of joint ventures, number of wives and transfers. Since this house is twelfth from Eighth (the house of death) it is also Marak house hence in the prediction of death its role is significant.

From this house problems related with urine, diabetes, lower abdominal disorders and gynecological cases are studied. Venus is the planet which is natural benefactor of the house.

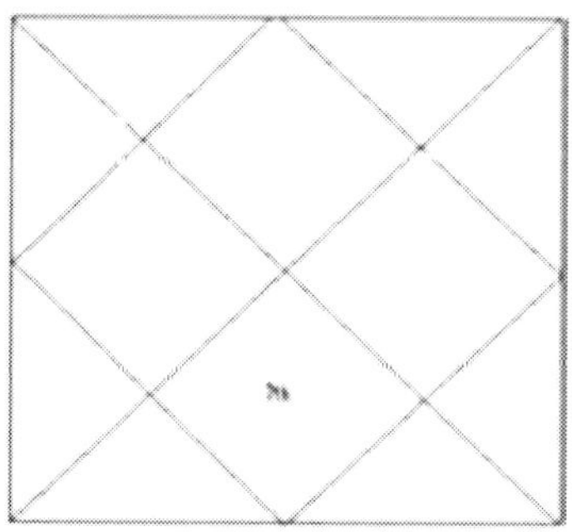

Eighth House

Known as *Randhra, Aayu, Mrityu, Vinash* etc. the eighth house is the second Trika bhava of a chart.

This house primarily signifies death, age, means of evading death, cause of death, fear of injuries, wealth of wife, secret wills, insurance, suicides, accidents, drowning, sufferings, defeats, disappointments, separation, and crematoriums etc. It is the signifier of wealth from secret means and interest in occult knowledge too.

Private problems, genital disease, hernia, boils, piles and indebtedness are considered from this house. Saturn is the natural causative planet of this house.

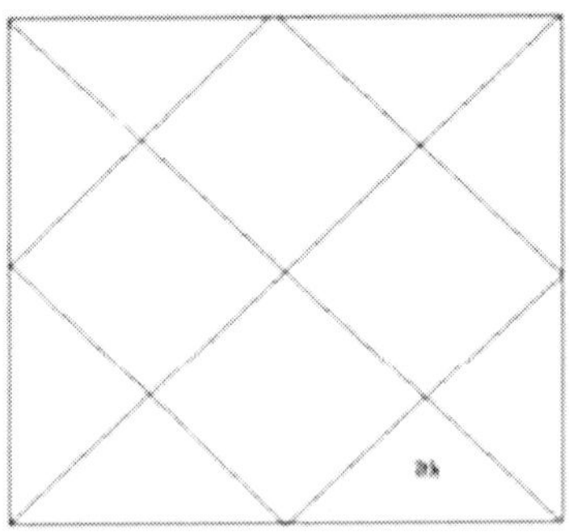

Ninth House

Dharam, Punya, Bhagya, Guru, Shubha, Tapa, Nava, Anka are the other names for the ninth house.

This house is of great importance since it is popularly called the house of fortune. Good the fortune less the hard work the person would require to do. There are people who get huge wealth from ancestors, wills, lotteries or sudden occurrences in their lives and lead royal life without even being worthy of it. Of what use hard work and struggle if it doesn't transform your fate. There are people who even after doing a lots of struggle fail to come over the things and this is fortune all about.

From this house we study religion, guru, faith, worship, long travels, foreign travels, wisdom, temples, places of worship and faith, meditation, philosophy, intuition, donations, philanthropy, sacrifice, higher education, law, telecommunications, humbleness etc. This house represents ailments relating with thighs, knees, menstrual disorders, gastric, and blood infections etc. Sun and Jupiter are the main benefactors of the ninth house.

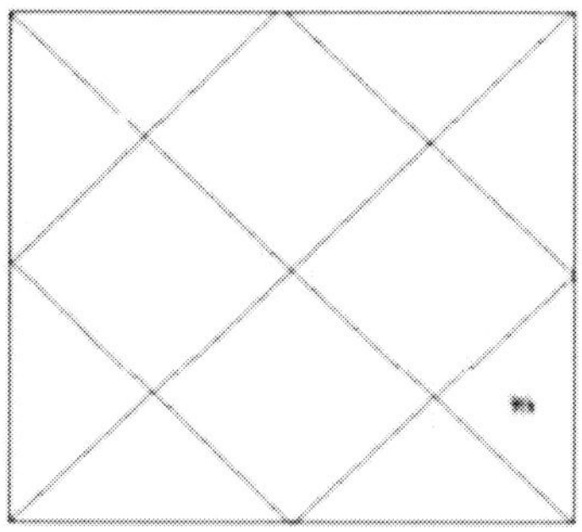

Tenth House

This house is also known by the names of Karam, Vyapaar, Rajya, Maan, Gyan etc.

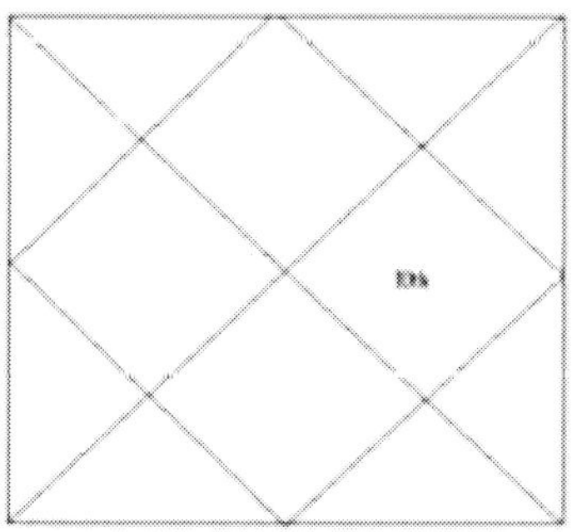

This house is the house of Karama, hence the things related with one's profession are reflected by it. From tenth house are observed profession, job, career, benefits from state, name, leadership, degrees , awards ,promotion, industry, success, rights, behavior, government, father, judge, horse riding and adoption.

This house represents diseases related with knee such as arthritis and disease like skin problems and gastritis etc. Sun, Mercury, Jupiter and Saturn are the prime benefactors of the tenth house.

Eleventh House

This is the house of income and also known as Bhava or Aaya sthan.

This house represents income from different sources, ambitions, optimism, vehicle, elder brother, friends, monetary benefits, lottery, education, son-in-law, daughter-in-law, promotion, luxuries, travels of father, and education of wife etc. This house represents the upper portion of foot. Hence, the injuries to foot, pindalies, fractures etc. are observed from this house. Jupiter represents the house as natural benefactor.

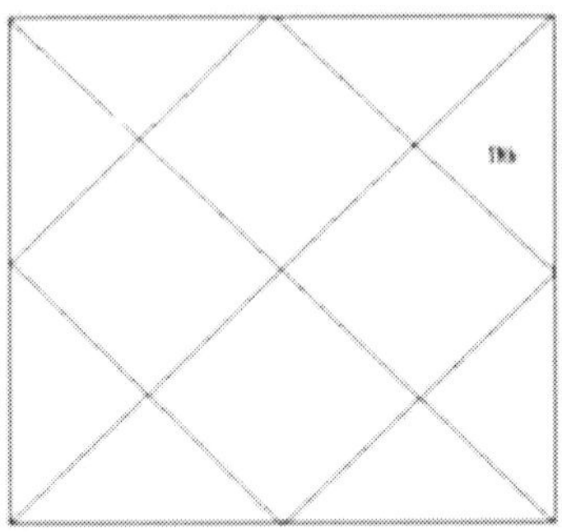

Twelfth House

This is the house of expenditure and it is also known as Vyaya sthan.

This is, although, the third Trika Stahan yet is of great

importance. It represents expenditure in any shape be it monetary or life, salvation, occult knowledge, foreign travels, spiritualism, imprisonment, donations, secret works, suicides, penalty, indebtedness, sufferings, deceit, rebellion, settlement in far off areas, poverty, misfortune, hospital, rest, scandals, raids, seamy side of life, illness of wife, uncle, morale of father, occupation of younger brother, problems of children, and travels of mother etc.

This house also represents the problems of left eye, feet, toes, left ear, allergy, polio and many such other diseases. Saturn is the sole benefactor of the house.

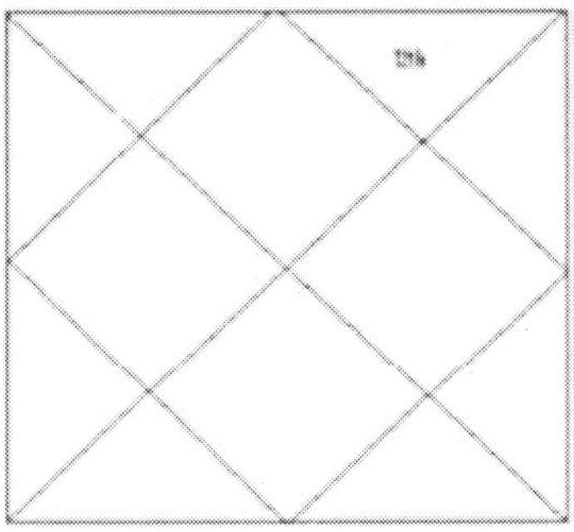

CHAPTER-6

Some Important Yogas

HARISH K THAKUR

Yoga, though simply stands for union of the two or more objects and in Hindu discipline for attaining union with the supreme spirit through intense meditation or concentration guided through regulating prescriptions of body postures, exercises and breathing etc.

In zodiac the union or clubbing of the planets (two or more) in a particular house forms a distinctive yoga deriving its virtues primarily from the properties of the planets, house (Bhava) of their residence, the natural owners of the house (Bhavesh), the natural benefactors of the house (Karkesh), the zodiac sign of that house and the planet that is the lord of the sign. In simple terms it is the complex whole of the positives and negatives derived from planetary positions, placements, signs of the houses and their lords and many more factors stated above that work accordingly on the life of the person under observation.

There are certain combinations which work quite effectively and at times miraculously, of course because of their multiplied prowess and strength. Mythological explications would call this a game of friends and enemies among the planets nine, of course the two being shadow planets. Of late there has evolved a trend of taking into account the role of four more far distant bodies like Hershel, Neptune, Pluto and Uranus. They might have impact on human personality like several other brighter bodies but their role when compared to the other nine stands quite feeble.

1. Digbal yoga

When six planets besides Saturn are placed in the houses of their comfort and prowess this yoga occurs. If in the horoscope of a person two planets occupy such places this yoga occurs partially and if three or more such planets furnish one's horoscope greater the strength of the yoga shall be. The person in whose horoscope such yoga takes place remains a potent, invincible, and indomitable person in life. He would lead a majestic life with great influence in public life. His rising to the higher public posts would not be a difficult thing. The placement of the planets in the houses of their comfort and prowess are as follows:

Sun	Tenth
Mercury	First (Lagna)
Mars	Tenth
Moon	Fourth
Venus	Fourth
Jupiter	First (Lagna)

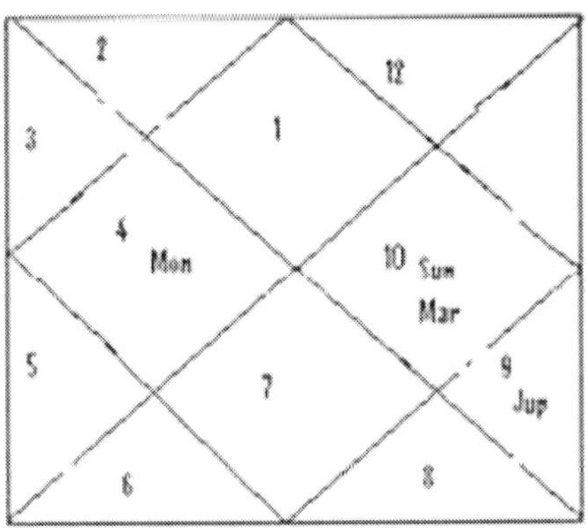

Table No. 1

2. Panch Mahapurusha Yogas

In both Indian and Western astrology the impact of five planets is considered immense especially when in Lagna they are placed in their own signs or the signs of their exaltation. Their placement in the other Kendra Bhavas (fourth, seventh and tenth house) also create the same yoga, though with little debilitation. They raise the status of the person to the newer heights with the definite tinge of the planet concerned. These planets are the Mercury, Mars, Jupiter, Venus and Saturn.

Strong Mercury, if placed in Virgo or Gemini Lagna constitutes Bhadra Yoga. Its location in fourth, seventh or tenth house in its own signs also constitute the same yoga. Since mercury represents mind, intelligence, skin etc. the native would have a healthy, tall and attractive figure. He will be known for sharp mind and will be good in mathematics and art. Such person is also known for powerful thinking, sharp wit and master of many arts, crafts and languages.

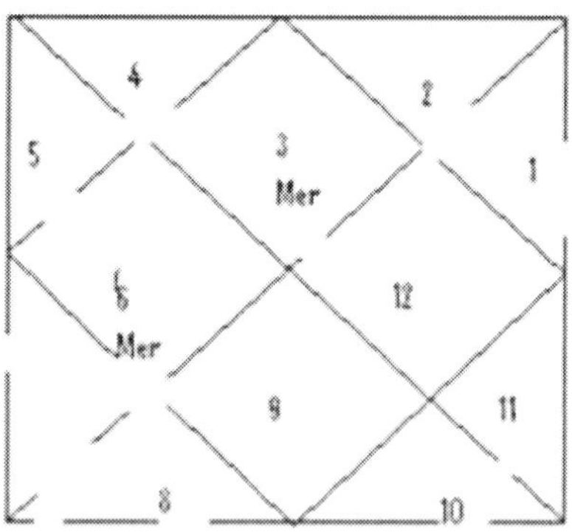

Strong Mars in Kendra Bhavas in Aries, Scorpio or Capricorn constitutes 'Ruchak Yoga', a yoga mostly desired by young people because of high morale, courage and energy that it gives. Mars is causative of fire and clashes since it is red in colour. It makes one egoist, high tempered, courageous, and quarrelsome. It brings success in the shape of high rank offices of forces (Army, Police, Navy, Air Force et.al.) (Table No 2)

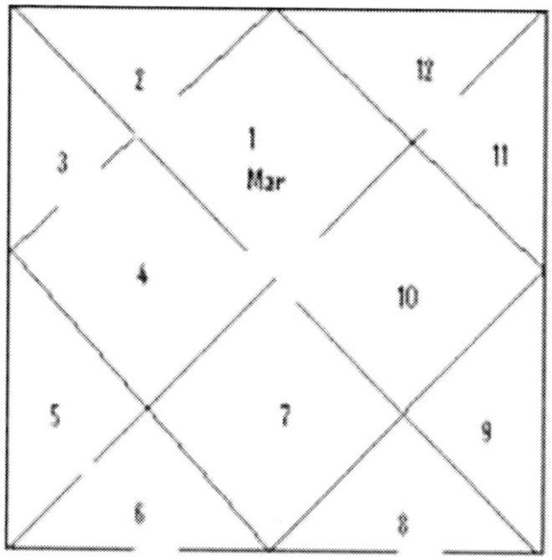

Table No. 2

The position of Jupiter in the Kendra bhavas in the signs of Sagittarius, Pisces or Cancer institute Hansa Yoga. The native of this yoga meets many good fortunes in life and is believed to lead a long comfortable life. The owner of this yoga leads a life like guru and earns very significant and venerated position in the society. He bears a fair, handsome, and healthy look with great devotion to parents, elders and teachers. It has been seen

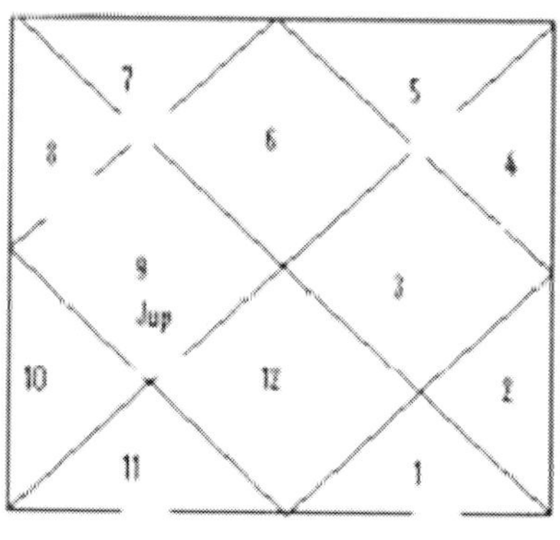

Table No. 3

that people having this yoga mostly become professors and teachers. Such people beg many honours from state and lead a long life. Jupiter in fourth house brings success from land, hotels, and cookery while in 10th house paves ways for financial benefits. Its location in 7th house causes benefits from partnerships or business. (Table No 3)

A strong Saturn in the signs of Capricorn, Aquarius or Libra in Kendra bhavas institutes Shasha Yoga. People owning this yoga usually bear wheatish or dark complexion with the element of honesty, sincerity, maturity and seriousness. These elements elevate the natives to higher social and political status because of greater public image and acceptability of them. Such people are deep investigators, researchers and are curious about the unraveled knowledge of the occult world. They sometimes develop problems with feet and limp while walking. Such natives mostly become researchers, surgeons, judges or engineers. (Table No 4).

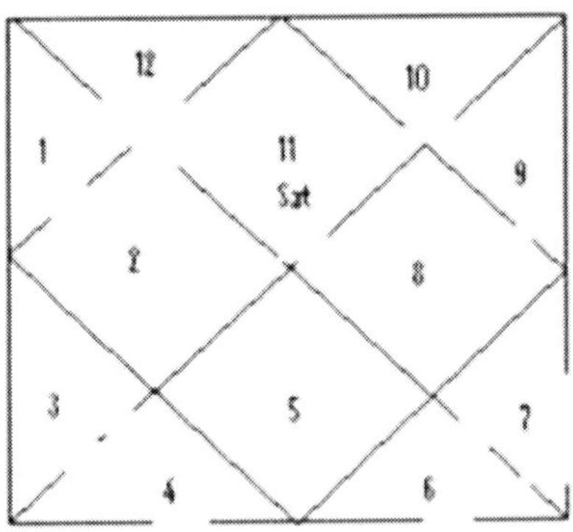

Table No. 4

Venus in Libra, Taurus or Pisces in the Kendra bhavas constitutes Malvya Yoga. This yoga gives natural beauty, good health and taste for poetry, art, music, literature, and luxurious things in life. Such natives are usually wealthy with good bungalows, vehicles and other amenities of life. The people of opposite sex are greatly attracted toward them. They are engaged in the professions of art, drama, acting, cosmetics, fashions, fabrics designing, and chemicals etc. Most of the cine stars, pop singers and musicians have well placed Venus in their charts. (Table No 5).

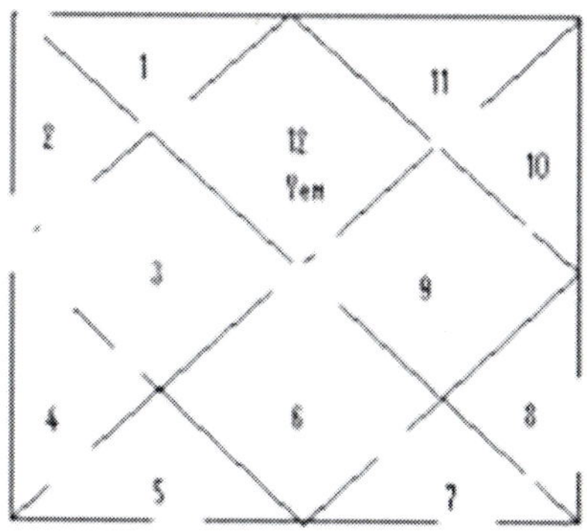

Table No. 5

3. Shubh Yoga

One simple way of adjudging the results of a chart are calculating from the very first house of the chart i.e. Lagna. If the Lagna is occupied by a benefic than obviously the good fortunes would

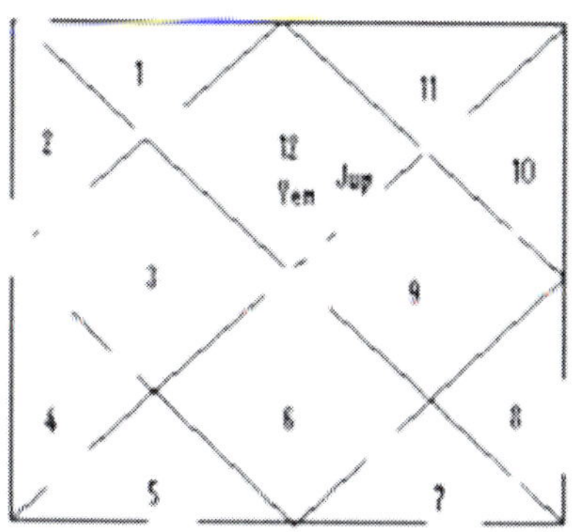

Table No. 6

be flowing to the incumbent. The nature and personality would be governed by the planet in occupation of the chart. However, one thing to be remembered here is the fact that the result should be concluded only after studying the features of the owner of the sign or the Rashi of the Lagna as well. (Table No 6)

4. Ashubh Yoga

Right against the above mentioned yoga is the yoga of misfortune, though, not necessarily too immense in negatives. If a malefic or a group of malefic planets occupies the Lagna than the natural qualities of such planets would impinge upon the personality of the incumbent. Here one thing is to be remembered again that if the owner of the sign placed in Lagna house is benefic i.e. Jupiter, Venus, Mercury or Moon then half of the negative effects are negated. The degree and the digbala (the natural power) of the planet are also to be taken into consideration here. This reminds one of the story of Hanuman. Malefic Saturn came into his life when Hanuman was battling Ravan's force. Hanuman was not phased out. He made Saturn enter his head. The latter kept wounding him, but that did not deter him from the battle royal. (Table No 7).

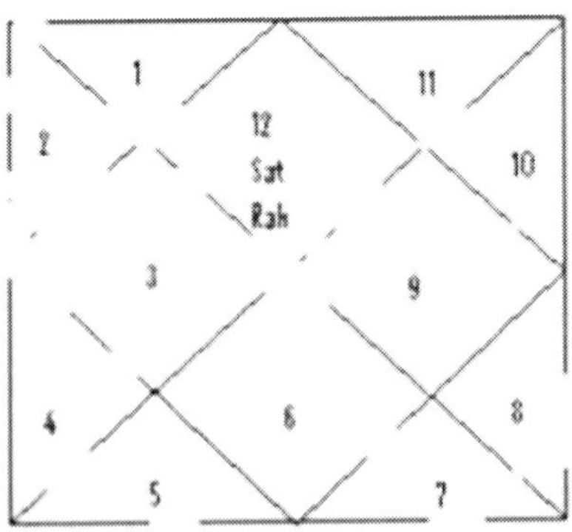

Table No. 7

5. Kavya Yoga (Muse)

Poetry is something that has to do with emotions, sentiments, and wisdom at the same time. The role of planets that are causative of love, emotion and wisdom therefore, becomes of utmost importance. Moon is the planet that makes one highly emotional and if it impresses upon Lagna, i.e. placed or aspects Lagna House or Lagnesh (the owner of the first house) the element of strong emotions governs the person. When this yoga is compounded by the wisdom of Jupiter and even Venus the emotions are transformed into letter. This happens when Jupiter aspects the Lagna or Lagnesh or when the Moon and the Jupiter sit together in Lagna or seventh house. The duo can aspect the Lagna or Lagnesh from different positions also. Gaj Kesari yoga is also additive to the flow of muse. It has been seen that if the house of Lagna is surrounded by Jupiter and Venus i.e. Jupiter in the second house and Venus in the twelfth (in Gemini Lagna) strong muse and scholasticism inspires the person. The creative talent of such persons gets expression more through muse and also in other genre of expression. (Table No 8)

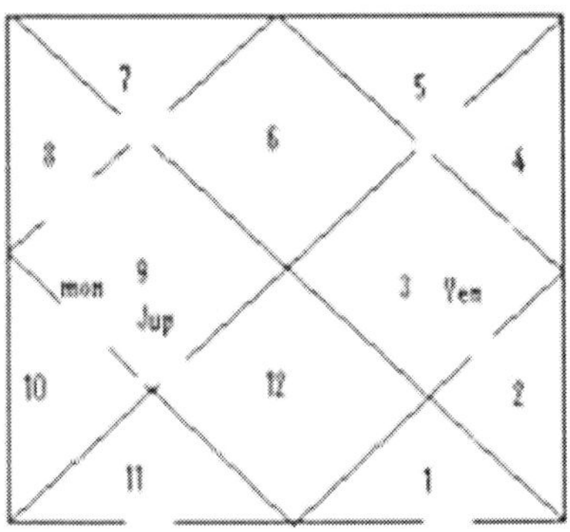

Table No. 8

6. Gaj Kesari Yoga (Jupiter-Moon Duad)

One of the most read and influential yoga in Indian astrology is the collaboration of Jupiter and the Moon. Jupiter is the planet of wisdom, intelligence and Gurudom but it also signifies the larger prosperity, name, popularity and good fortune in one's life. While Moon represents emotions and motherhood it also signifies knowledge and mind. Since the fourth House also represents knowledge, mind, land and motherhood Jupiter plays a significant role here. The combination of the two, therefore, brings greater fortunes in the shape of prosperity, popularity, scholasticism, and benefits from state. It has been seen that this yoga occurs quite frequently in the horoscopes of scholars, eminent writers, professors, officers, and teachers in general.

Even the combination of Sun and Jupiter is also considered to form Gaj Kesari Yoga ensuring success in public sphere. (Table No 9)

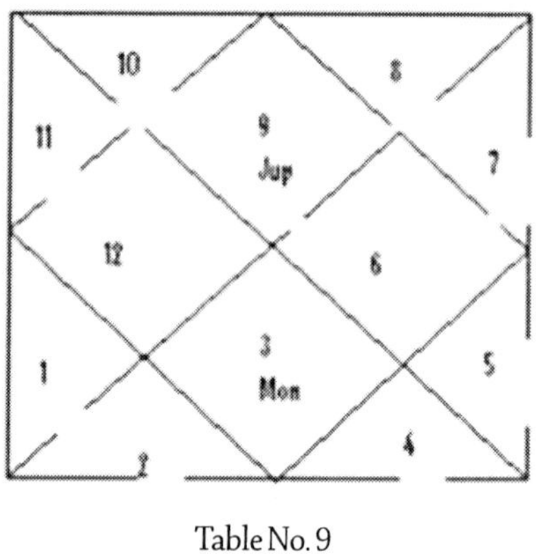

Table No. 9

7. Ruler Yoga (Raj Yoga)

In the Lagna Chart the ninth and tenth houses are considered the most powerful houses since they represent the houses of fortune and profession. It is only good fortune that makes profession fruitful and glorifying and if the ninth house is under the influence of malefic planets the majesty of the tenth house loses most of its worth. It has been studied that Sun and Jupiter play a significant role in the tenth house provided the ninth house is well embellished i.e. owned or aspected by the natural owner, or owner of the house. Sun and Mars alone, if exalted or in their own sign, can lift the professional career of a person. Whereas, Sun brings benefits from the State in the shape of high ranking officers, honours and favours, Mars leads to success in sports and forces.

The other combination of houses, which is second to the combination of ninth and tenth, is the one of fourth and fifth house. Placement of Moon or Jupiter in the fourth and Mercury or Saturn in the fifth gives special strength to the chart of the native.

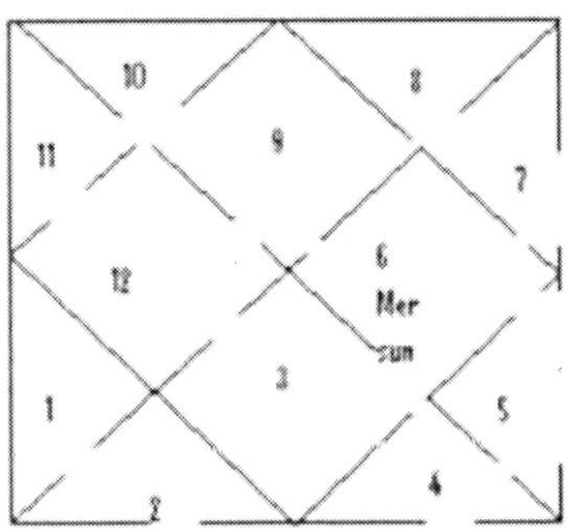

Table No. 10

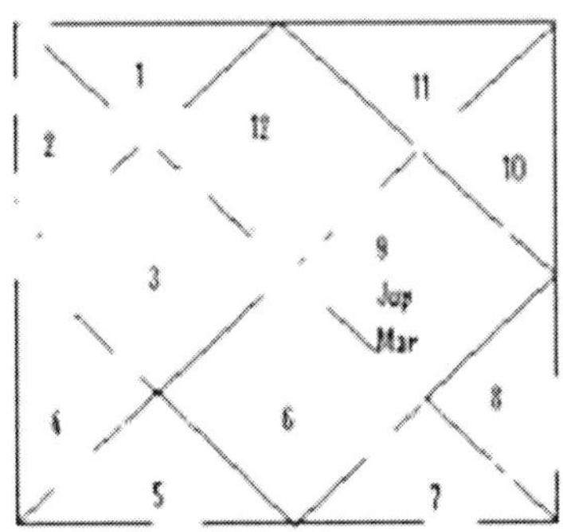

Table No. 11

Sometimes the owners of the signs of these two combinations exchange places i.e. the owner of the sign of ninth sits in the tenth and the owner of the sign of the tenth sits in the ninth house. This exchange of places is considered Raj Yogkarka and the native rises to great heights in life.

Then there are a large number of combinations and placements of planets in different houses and signs which strengthen the charts of the people differently making up for the Raj Yoga. (Table No 10 & 11)

8. Yogas Related to Adjacency with Sun and Moon

Then there are certain yogas which emanate from their placement in the vicinity of Sun or Moon i.e. in the same house as that of Sun or moon or in the house that falls second or twelfth to the Sun or moon. Such yogas which relate to the second house after the Sun or the Moon are considered more helpful and positive because of the natural value of the second house, i.e. family, wealth and oratory. While calculating the exactness of the results out of such placements it should be kept in mind that if there are more than one or two planets placed in the said positions then the results would be mixed according to the characteristics of each planet. In the calculation of these yogas from the perspective of Sun and Moon the presence of each one against the other is not taken into account i.e. in the case of Sun related yogas the role of Moon is not considered and vice versa.

9. Veshi Yoga

If any planet with the exception of moon is placed in the second house from the Sun this yoga takes place. This yoga occurs as per the characteristics of the planets that follow Sun in the second house.

If the planet is benefic good fortunes would flow to the person and if the planet is malefic like Rahu, Saturn or Mars the person would be trapped by misfortunes like bad company and poverty. It has been seen that the following of Sun by Venus and Jupiter brought a great deal of success to the bearers of such charts. The charts of many popular personalities like that of Mahatma Gandhi, Subhash Chandra Bose, Rabindranath Tagore and Vir Sarvarkar are witness to this yoga which made them immensely popular and successful among masses. (Table No 12 & 13).

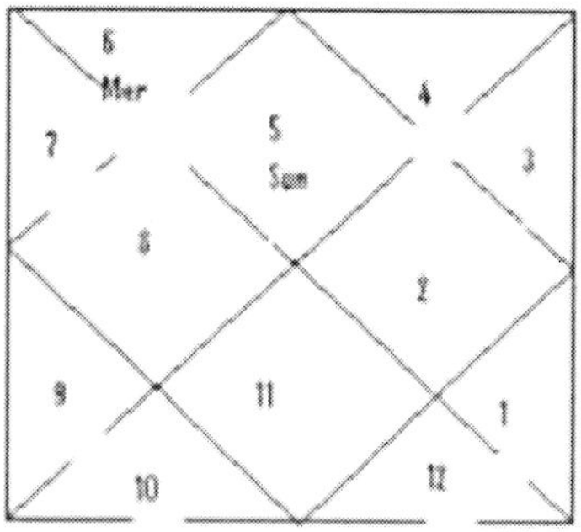

Table No. 10

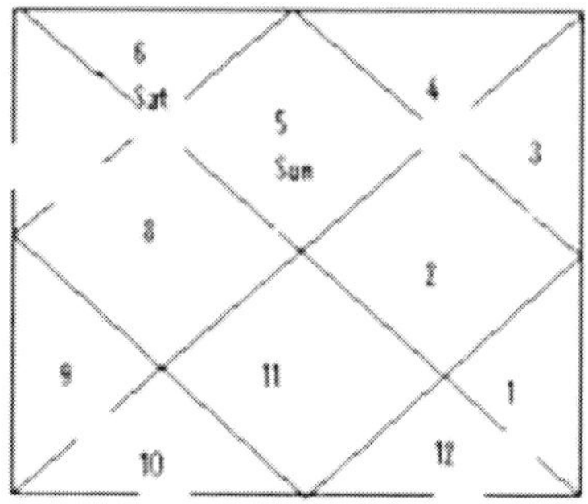

Table No. 11

10. Vaasi Yoga

This yoga takes place when any of the planet leaving moon aside settles in the twelfth house from the Sun. Again the results largely depend on the nature of the planet placed. Malefic planets mostly cause estrangement from family and settle one at distant places from the motherland. However, benefic planets give one the virtue of dexterity at work and make the person highly successful, happy, extravagant and benevolent. (Table No 14).

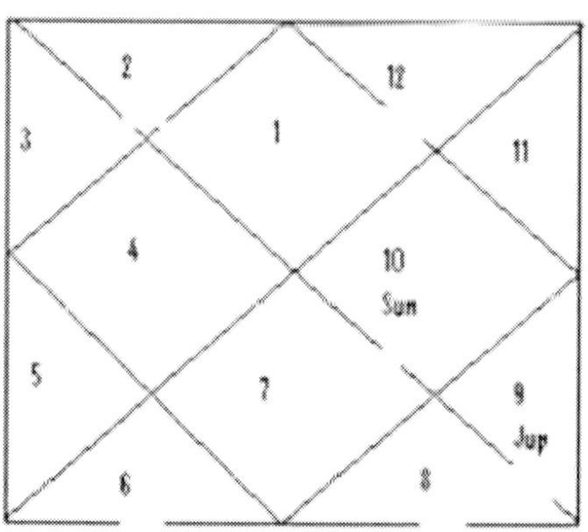

Table No. 14

11. Ubhayacharik Yoga

This yoga occurs when both the houses from the Sun i.e. second and the twelfth are occupied by planets. Again the result depends on the nature of the planets. If the benefic planets sit on these houses the incumbent then develops great powers of adjudication, judgment, forbearance, tolerance, eloquence and debate. Such people become good sports persons, Judges, lawyers and get benefits from state.

But, if the malefic planets acquire the abovementioned houses than the result could be overturned by the characteristics of these planets. In such acquisitions the role of moon is not taken into account. (Table No 15)

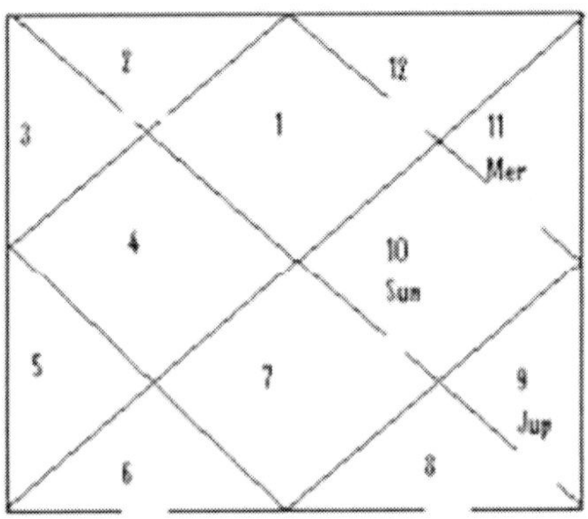

Table No. 15

12. Sunfa Yoga

If the second house counted from Moon is occupied by any planet other than Sun than this yoga takes place. This yoga makes one hardworking and dexterous in the area of profession. The profession and the source of income that incumbent relies upon are determined by the nature of the planets that occupy the second house from the sun. For example Jupiter takes one to the field of education, officialdom and wisdom, Mercury to commerce, art and religion, Mars to sports, forces and valour and Venus to films, art and vehicles. (Table No 16).

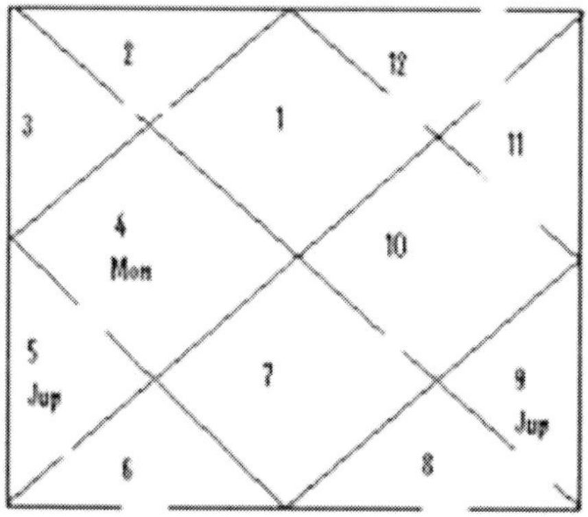

Table No. 16

13. Anfa Yoga

When the twelfth house from the Moon is occupied by a planet other than Sun, Anfa Yoga occurs. This yoga is again determined by the nature of the occupant of the house. Benefic planets bring beauty, humility, and magnetism to the personality of the incumbents whereas the malefic planets give opposite qualities to the person. (Table No 17).

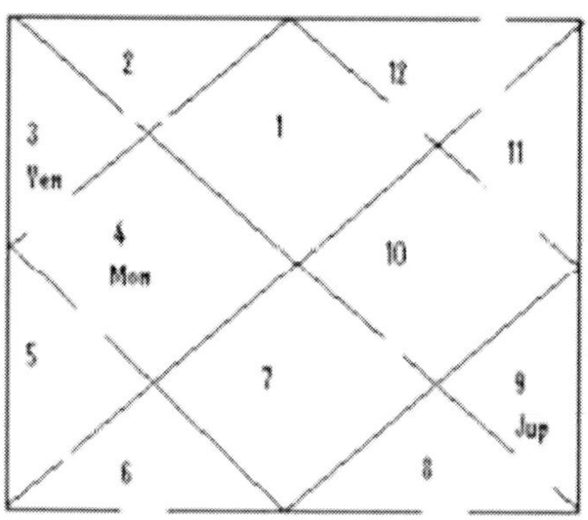

Table No. 17

14. Durdhara Yoga

Very much like Ubhayacharik Yoga Durdhara yoga takes place in relation to Moon. When Moon is surrounded by two planets this yoga takes place. The person born under this yoga earns all fame, wealth and rises to high public life. (Table No 18)

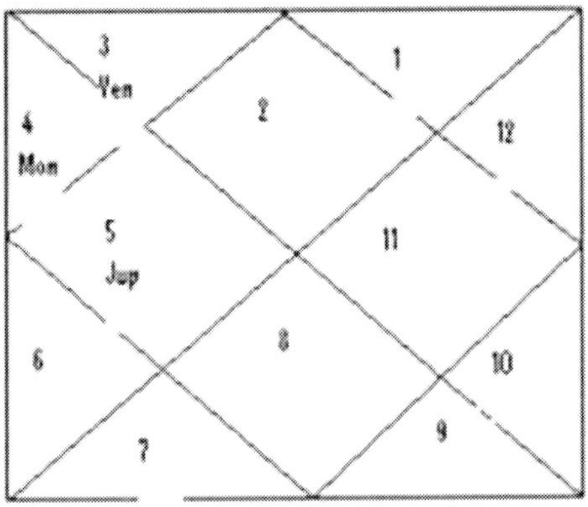

Table No. 17

15. Kemdrum Yoga

If the second and the twelfth house from the Moon are empty and not occupied by any planet than Kemdrum yoga occurs. This is one of the most unwanted yoga since it causes resourcelessness, poverty, unemployment and estrangement from happiness in life. Such people are always dependent on the help of others. The married life of such people also keeps disturbed because of unfavourable family circumstances.

There are many beliefs about the non-occurrence of this yoga because of the different aspects over Moon and placement of Moon in certain places like Kendra sthan etc. It is also observed that if Moon is placed with certain other planets than Kemdrum yoga gets weakened. (Table No 19)

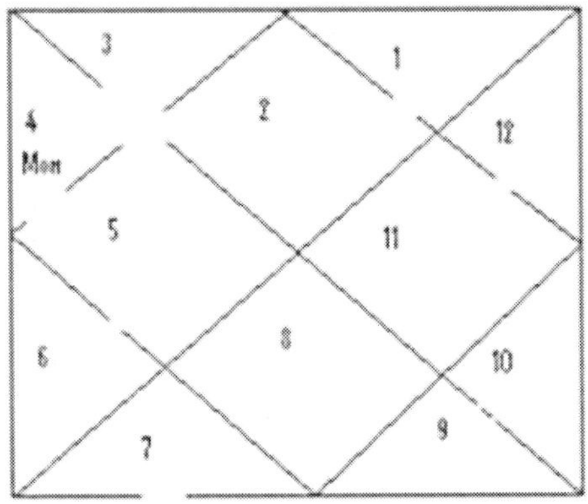

Table No. 18

16. Daridra Yoga

Another sister yoga to Kemdrum yoga is Daridra (poverty) yoga which happens when all the Kendra Sthan (Squires) are empty or occupied by malefic planets from the Moon or Lagna house.

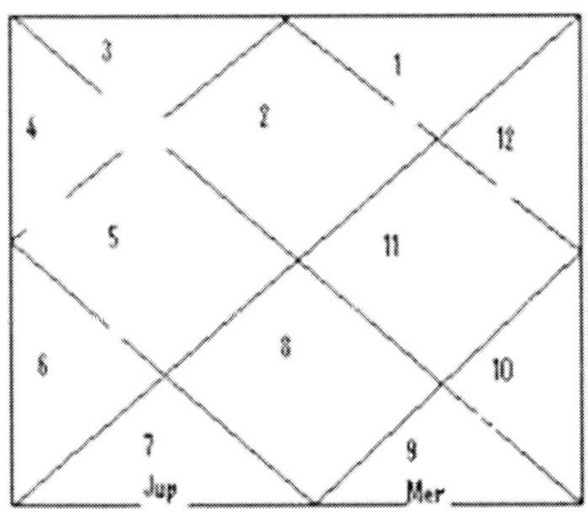

Table No. 20

Since charts are also interpreted from Moon and Sun except Lagna the weakened Moon or Sun or their being aspected by debilitated planets also lead to such kind of yoga. This yoga also happens in different ways for example the owners of eleventh (house of income) or second house (house of wealth) are placed in trika sthan i.e. 3rd, 6th and 8th houses. Sometimes it has been seen that even after having good position of owners of 11th or 2nd house the incumbent remains pauper because of his 9th house being under the influence of malefic planets. (Table No 20)

17. Chaamar Yoga (Yoga of high wisdom)

This yoga takes place when the Lagnesh is in the sign of its exaltation in the Kendra Sthan and is aspected by Jupiter. The person bearing this equation is the owner of high intellect, famous and successful in life. (Table No 21)

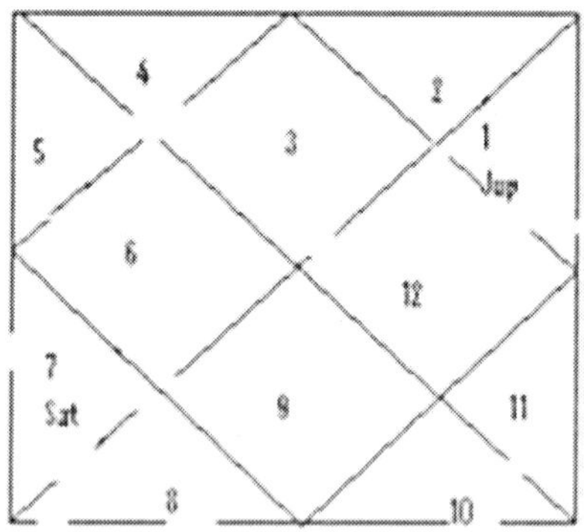

Table No. 21

18. Jaya Yoga

If the owner of the sixth house is in the sign of debilitation and the owner of the tenth house (the house of profession) is exalted than Jay Yoga takes place. The incumbent bearing this yoga turns mostly invincible in life. This yoga gets more strengthened if the owner of 6th house is Sun and the owner of 10th house is Jupiter. (Pisces lagan-sun in 8th n Jupiter 5th, Table No 22)

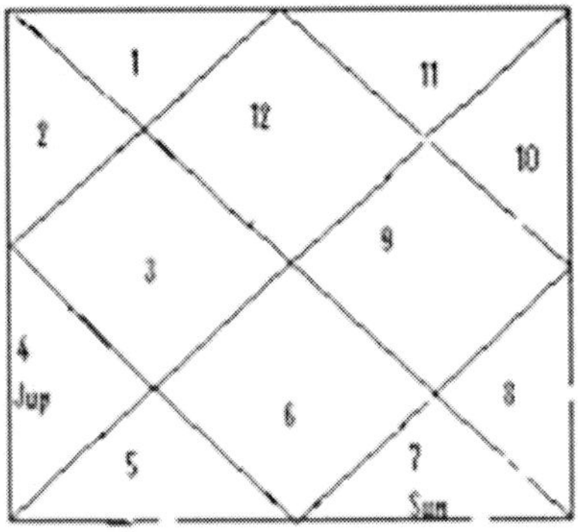

Table No. 22

19. Shubhakartri Yoga and Papkartri Yoga

This yoga is said to be occurring in two ways. If the Lagna House is surrounded by benefic planets (in the 12th and 2nd house) shubhakrtri yoga takes place and if these houses are occupied by malefic planets, then Papkartri Yoga takes place. As is obvious from the yoga if Lagna is surrounded by benefic planets than shubhkartri yoga occurs and if Lagna is surrounded by malefic planets than papkartri yoga takes place. It should be kept in mind that the results are different or mixed if the Lagna is surrounded by both kinds of planets. (Table No 23 & 24)

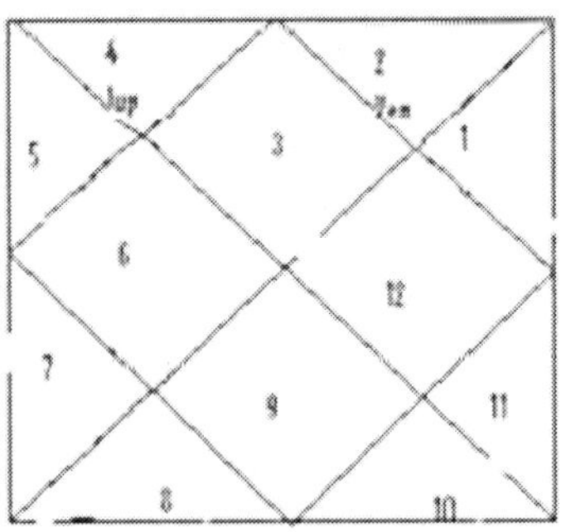

Table No. 23

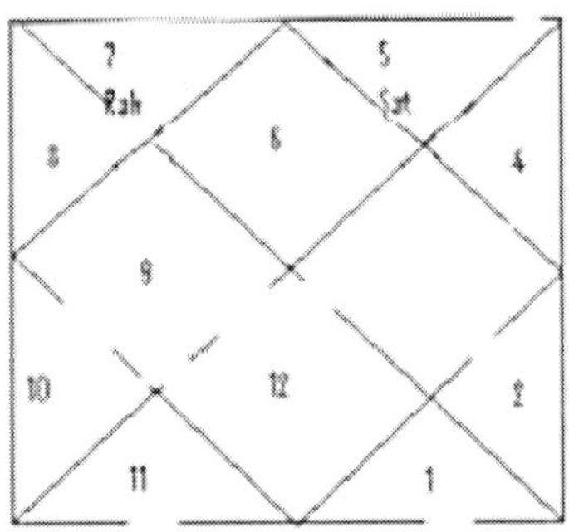

Table No. 24

20. Khadag Yoga

This yoga is said to be one of the raj yoga so far as it gives immense rise in life to the person under influence. This yoga also gives scholasticism of many fields and makes one valorous and adventurous in life. This yoga occurs when the owner of the ninth house (house of fortunes) occupies the second house (house of wealth) and the owner of the second house is placed in the ninth house. Besides this the lagnesh, the owner of the lagna sign, should be placed in the Kendra bhava (squires). (Table No 25).

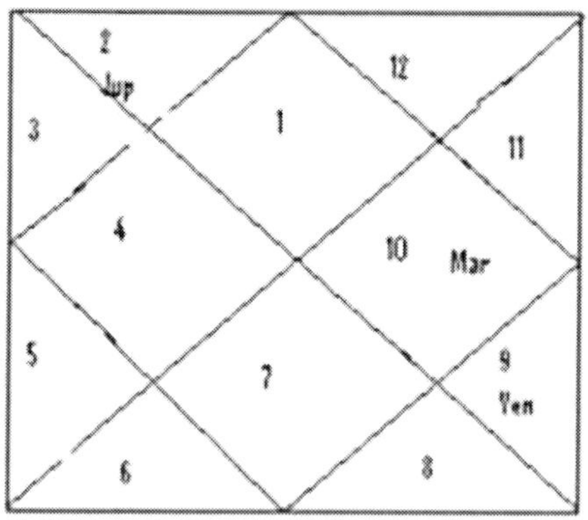

Table No. 25

21. Chandradhi Yoga

Chandradhi yoga takes place when the sixth, seventh or eighth house counted from Moon are occupied by benefic planets like Mercury, Jupiter or Venus. It is not necessary that all the houses should be occupied by the planets rather occupation of any one of them also causes Chandradhi yoga. The reason behind the yoga seems to be the turning of the malefic influence of the said houses into benefic one by the positive power of the planets of good fortunes. (Table No 26)

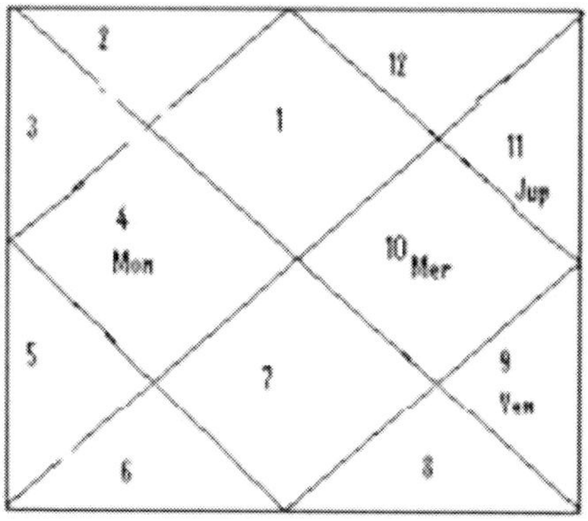

Table No. 26

22. Laxmi Yoga

Very much like the name of the yoga this yoga is causative of immense wealth and happiness in life. Since second house is the house of wealth, bank balance and happiness of the family this yoga definitely takes this house into consideration. This yoga mostly takes place with the change of houses by the owners of second and ninth house. It is also believed that if Lagnesh is strong and the owner of the ninth house is in the Kendra bhava in its own sign or the sign of exaltation Laxmi yoga happens. (Table No 27).

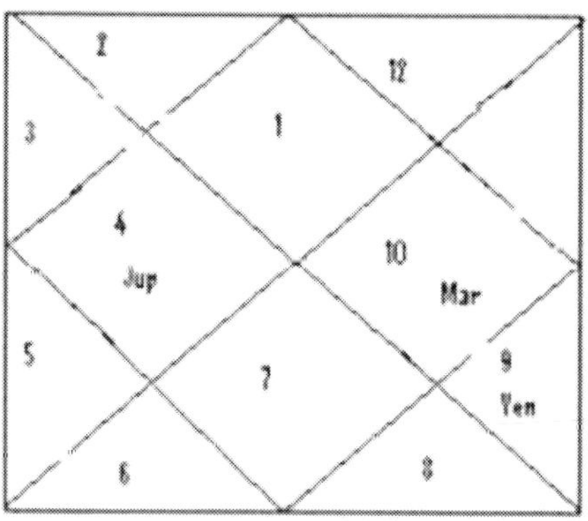

Table No. 27

23. Chandra-Mangal Yoga

If the two planets Moon and Mars sit together in a chart this yoga takes place. It has both benefic and malefic influences as per the equations of the chart. The joining together of moon and mars in second, ninth, tenth and eleventh house is considered most benefic. While reading the chart it should also be observed whether the two planets bear executive force (karkesh) in the chart or not. For example this yoga occurs strongly in the charts of Aries, Cancer, Scorpio and Pisces. Positively this yoga gives great happiness, wealth and fame in life. Such people are quite popular among women also. In the adverse position this yoga causes frictions in relations with mother, wife and leads to illicit ways of earning. (Table No 28).

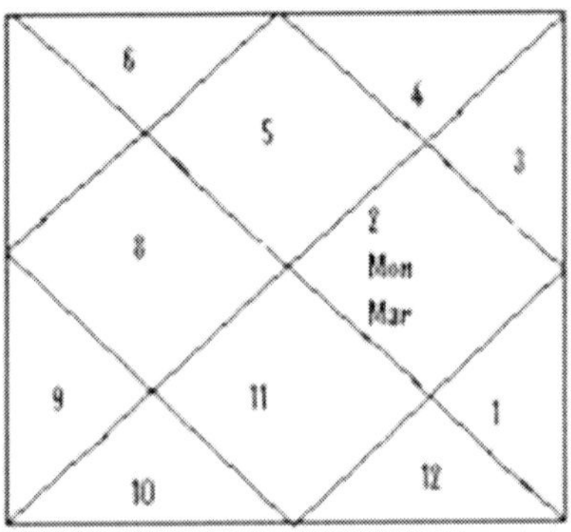

Table No. 28

24. Kusum Yoga

The zodiac signs are broadly categorized into three types- Sthir (Stable), Dwi-swabhav (of Dual character) and Chala (movable or instable). If the Kendrasthan of a chart belongs to the signs of first kind (Taurus, Leo, Scorpio & Aquarius) and Venus is placed in square, Saturn in house number ten and moon in triangle then occurs a yoga called Kusum Yoga. This yoga makes one benevolent and famous in life. (Table No 29).

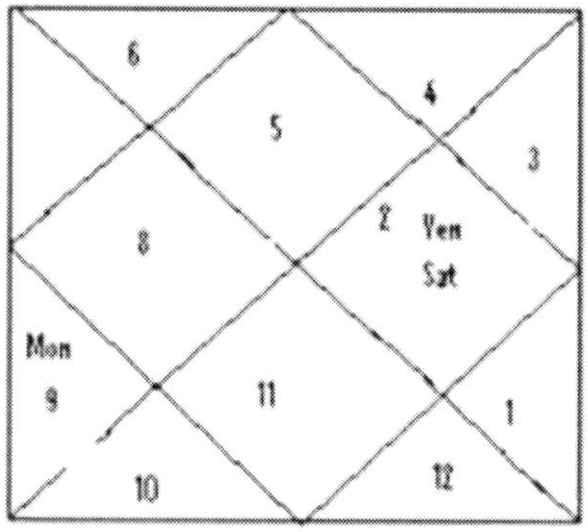

Table No. 29

25. Shakat Yoga

Shakat yoga happens when Jupiter is placed in sixth, eighth or twelfth house (Trika) from the house of moon. This yoga is symbolic of misfortunes, unhappiness and unsteadiness in life. The chart number 30 shows how Jupiter is placed in the 6th house and is 6th from moon which is placed in the Lagna house in the sign of Taurus. (Table No 30).

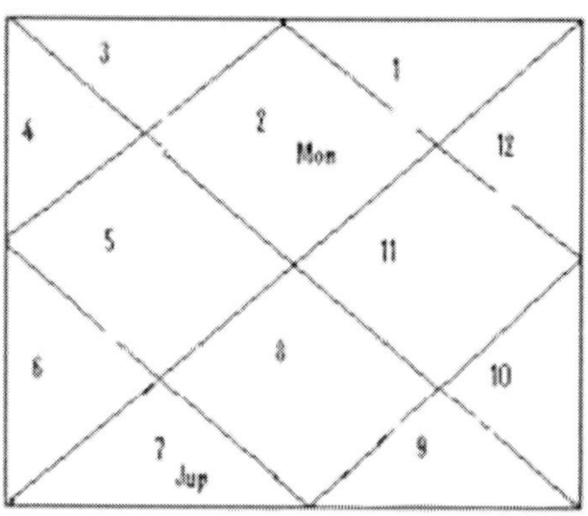

Table No. 30

26. Yogas of Illness and Accidents

There are hundreds of planetary combinations and placements which act against the health and fate of man. However, while predicting about them one has to observe the chart from multiple of angles and dimensions. Here are some important diseases and accidental equations:

Blindness

Sun and Venus are considered the two prime bodies behind the sight of man. When these planets are affected by the debilitated or negative planets diseases relating to eye might occur.

A Debilitated Sun or Moon in the twelfth house

B Weak Venus in the twelfth house or in the lagna

C In the Leo Lagna the Sun and the Moon together aspected by Mars or Saturn

D Sun, Moon and Venus are in the Trik sthana (6th, 8th, & 12th)

E Sun together with Moon or Venus or Lagnesh is placed in the Trika Sthan.

F The second and twelfth houses being occupied or aspected debilitated Sun, Mars or Saturn

G Moon aspected by Saturn and the Sun is placed with Rahu

H Weak Saturn, Mars or Moon in the twelfth house.

I Sun or Moon in the seventh house in the signs of Leo or cancer aspected by malefic Mars

Dumbness

A Debilitated Mercury aspected by Saturn or Mars in the second House

B Second house of the chart being occupied by malefic

planets and a weak Mercury

C The owner of the sixth house is placed with Mercury

D Mercury together with Jupiter is placed in Trika Sathan

E The sign of Taurus is occupied by malefic planets and a weak Moon or Mercury

F Mercury in the water signs (Cancer, Scorpio and Pisces) aspected by feeble Moon

G The owner of the second house together with Jupiter is placed in the Trika Bhavas

Yogas of Infirmities

A Moon aspected by Saturn and mars in the sign of scorpio or Cancer

B Saturn and Mars in the sixth house aspecting the Lagnesh (owner of the Ascendant sign)

C Saturn, Mars and the lagnesh in the Trika bhavas

D Saturn and the mars in the sixth house aspected by Rahu

E Mars and Jupiter in the sixth and twelfth house and the weak lagnesh

F Moon in the sign of Cancer aspected by debilitated Saturn, Mars or Rahu

G Saturn and Mars in the sixth house affected by Rahu

I Sun, Moon and Saturn in the eighth house

J Owner of the sixth house sits in conjunction with ascendant and aspected by debilitated malefic planets. More the number of malefic planets greater the chance of mutilated constitution.

Miscellaneous Diseases and Accidents

In most of the cases of external injuries to the body of man the role of Sun, Mars, Saturn, Rahu and Ketu is take into consideration. While Sun represents the bones, Mars represents the muscles, Rahu poison and Ketu the fire.

A The combination of Mars and Ketu has been found one of the prime cause behind accidents. Its presence in Lagna, sixth, seventh, eighth or tenth house can cause exernal injuries to men

B Mars and Ketu in any of the above houses affecting Lagna and aspected by weak Saturn can cause accident out of fire, explosion or crash.

C Ascendant and Mars are placed in the trika bhavas

D The karkesh (natural benefic of the house) of the sixth house is placed in the eighth house in conjunction with Moon or Sun or Mercury the chances of injury to face, head or chest are more.

E If Lagnesh is trapped between two malefic planets or Moon is compressed between two malefic planets in Aries or Scorpio or in Capricorn or Aquarius different situations of mishappenings arise according to the characteristics of planets, Bhavas and zodiac signs.

F Weak moon aspected by malefic planets in the Lagna or placed in the eighth house is causative of drowning.

G Rahu and Lagnesh in the Lagna or trika Bhavas, Moon and Mercury in the Trika bhavas lead to infections, infectious diseases or poisoning.

H Exalted mercury in the sixth house aspected by the malefic planets; Saturn, Mars, Moon and Venus in the Trika bhavas; Mercury, Moon, Mars and Saturn in the signs of Aries or Taurus or Mercury, Moon and Lagnesh with Rahu or Ketu are causative of skin problems or leprosy.

CHAPTER-7

The Song of Stones
An Introduction to Crystals

NAMITA SETHI

The word crystal comes from the Greek word krustallos which mean " ice" and "rock crystal". As defined in a Wikipedia entry, a crystal or crystalline solid is a material whose ions, atoms or molecules are arranged in a highly ordered microscopic structure, forming a crystal lattice that extends in all directions. Most have flat faces with indentations, inclusions (of one or more minerals) and characteristic orientations. The same Wiki entry lists crystal therapy as a pseudo-scientific practice.

This section on crystals makes no claims to be a scientifically established study, except when discussing mineral components. Studying and working with crystals is a purely intuitive practice for self- satisfaction and evolution. Where any therapeutic benefits are listed they are not to be taken as prescriptive in any way and should never be a substitute for medical advice from a qualified practitioner. Nor are the crystals I discuss to be used as gem stone remedies as prescribed by an astrologer. There are significant differences from an astrological approach in my study. Crystals discussed in this section are usually not very expensive. They can be used in their raw (rock) form, tumbled, in small pieces or as jewellery. They are not as refined and focussed on a specific effect as gem stones. Not all are stones either. Amber is a resin, Obsidian is volcanic glass, Petrified Wood is fossilized wood, Rudraksha is a bead from a tree and Tektites are believed to have come from space and not of this earth at all. The most significant difference is that when using a crystal one must not look at the birth chart or a description on the internet (though these have their uses) but rely solely on one's intuition.

At different times we may find different crystals useful. Our needs evolve constantly as our emotions and circumstances shift and we make a conscious attempt to raise our consciousness. A crystal may affect other people differently than you and will also feel different to you at different times. So how do they work and how do we know if they are of any "use" to us?

There are very good books on crystals that explain their structure, effects, metaphysical properties and details of how they have been used in healing in different civilizations of the past including the Egyptian, Native- American, Chinese, Tibetan, Indian, Roman, Celtic, Mayan and Aztec cultures during different historical periods. I have found the books of Naisha Ahsian, Robert Grienger, Cassandra Eason, Sue and Simon Lily, and Judy Hall very useful. However, my own experience with crystals has taught me that one should not just buy and wear a crystal blindly because a book or website recommends it. Quite a few authors have done their research thoroughly and have channelled some of this information from their spirit guides but it may not be applicable to the reader always. Mining and selling of crystals is big business and many shops will sell worthless plastic and baubles in the name of Feng- shui and crystal therapy.

What I recommend is that you hold a crystal, play with it, gaze at it and see how you feel about it. Some people can instantly feel a different vibe from a piece of glass, quartz (sphatik), a plastic bead and say a high vibrational stone like Selenite. After-all, all objects radiate energy: only the energy signature is different. But most people may not register anything immediately. It does not matter. If crystals attract you, it might be a good idea to visit a crystal shop or website and just look at different pieces and study them calmly without any urgency or expectation. In my experience the colour or crystal that calls out to you is the one you need at that moment. And after you have "worked" with a crystal or had it around in your space for a while, revisit the shop and see if something different catches your eye, because having been with a crystal, say clear quartz, will have already shifted something in the aura and increase sensitivity to your next crystal.

Readers must also note that by itself a crystal is dormant. No crystal can work any magic on you unless you set an intention and programme it. The crystal will aid working on our inner issues only if we want to. Say for example, a person decides to wear an Amethyst or Turquoise to deal with alcohol addiction issues. It will be an inert piece of jewellery till one meditates with the stone and sets this intention for it. Wearing crystals or being near them does shift our energy and that of the room we are in. They can encourage serendipity: the chance of being at the right place at the right time and attracting just what you need for your growth at a certain time in your life. But the reader must try this out for themselves and not believe the author blindly.

Crystals can be used as a stepping stone in one's spiritual evolution but most people will eventually outgrow using them as a tool. Energy healers use crystals to empower, direct or assist healing but no one needs to be dependent on them, at least not for long. They are best used as a medium of self-realization and intuitive awareness. Nor do we need to buy very expensive or rare crystals or high vibration crystals. For example, most kinds of quartz (clear, rose, amethhyst, citrine, smoky) are very powerful and versatile and easily available in India.

One can just meditate on a stone or crystal by looking at its picture and it starts working if the intention is there. Some crystals one may find soothing and calming, some stimulating, some helpful for increasing focus, some to take one into a trance, some just to bring peace and harmony in a space, some for peaceful sleep, some to help heal traumas, some for protection. Some storeowners keep crystals in certain areas to unconsciously influence a shopper to buy more (which I think is manipulative!).

Thus, these articles offer general observations which must always be substantiated by the user's individual experience. If holding a Moldavite or keeping a certain crystal on your third eye gives you headache or dizziness, do not use it. Unlike most authors, I do not recommend placing crystals in water and drinking gem elixirs because it may contain something toxic like lead. You never know so better safe than sorry. Nor is it a good idea to use crystals to forcibly awake or move Kundalini. That is what a good Guru is for, else leave it well alone. Use a crystal that makes you feel positive, that attracts you and changes things for the better. There is no substitute for patience and observation.

Crystals can absorb negative energy so they need to be cleansed regularly especially when they just arrive from the shop. Some need more cleansing than others. There are various methods for cleansing as by using running water, water from a natural source like a mountain river, placing them in sea salt, running incense smoke over them, placing them in a bowl full of unrefined/ brown rice, soil or using healing sounds (see section below). Salt and water can scratch many crystals. A crystal like Celestite will just crumble in your hands and self -destruct if you leave it in water. As one becomes more attuned to one's crystal/s, one can tell when they need cleansing. The next step is charging under moonlight. Some crystals like sunlight but not all do. Amethyst and Celestite lose colour and fade when placed under direct sunlight. The most important part of charging is to set an intention. Some examples of positive affirmations are: "Let Love and Light surround me in a protective bubble", "May only that which is for my highest good be brought into my ambit", "This crystal will protect me from those who drain my energy", "I attract abundance", or " I will now focus on my studies with renewed vigour" etc.

Never use a crystal or send out a negative thought to harm anyone. The energy we send out into the world is what comes back to us. Keep your affirmations positive and let crystals help you attract abundance, joy, positivity, good friends, resolution to conflicts, enhanced meditation and energy and good health.

Should you buy crystals? Only if you want to study them and feel driven to know, understand and change yourself. There are no quick fixes in life. The journey of self-knowledge is its own reward. We cannot change people or control them (and we should not want to). When we start working on ourselves, magic happens. Change manifests outside of ourselves, transforming our lives and our environment in profound ways. This in turn affects our health, addressing imbalances, our work and personal lives and helps us realize our connection with the Universe, all that exists and divine energy. Crystals are our allies on this path.

The role of crystals in balancing emotions and regulating the state of the human mind is well known. All crystals impact the mind and emotions though the exact effect varies from one individual to another and also for the same person from one moment to another. Crystals need to be cleansed regularly and scrupulously because they absorb negative energy. The most popular method of cleansing crystals is to wash them with sea salt and water. However, quite a few crystals are fragile. Smudging with sage or incense is another widely adopted method. After cleansing, crystals are charged in sunlight and moonlight. Some crystals like amethyst and Celestite lose their colour in sunlight.

Clearing the Energy of Crystals with Sound

As a general rule its best to keep most coloured crystals away from direct sunlight. Some people like to cleanse and charge all their crystals and jewellery by placing it on a clear quartz cluster. This is a convenient option because quartz can easily be cleaned with salty water, spring water or running water and be kept in sunlight as well. However, clear quartz can catch fire if placed for long under strong sunlight so one must be careful.

Another method of cleansing crystals as well as our own energies and those of certain spaces (home/office/study/alter/car) is to use the healing frequencies of different sounds. The mind produces certain number of waves per second depending on the state of stimulation or relaxation at that moment. Deep sleep or meditation corresponds to delta waves, light or early sleep and meditation and relaxation correspond to alpha waves and the usual alert and awake state corresponds to beta waves. By playing with varying frequencies the brain can be brought into certain states. Binaural beats, for instance, play a different frequency to the right ear and the left ear (this is clearly heard with headphones). The difference in the frequency translates into number of beats per second (Hertz) in our hearing perception. For example if the left ear hears 528 Hz and the right 524 Hz per second, we will hear four beats per second. This is the principle behind using binaural beats to induce a relaxed and meditative state of mind. This was well known in the Himalayas and Tibetan singing bowls are a testimony to the magical effects of multiple frequencies that are emitted one after the other. In Tibetan Buddhist practice singing bowls are used to begin and end periods of silent meditation .the best bowls are traditionally handmade and produce harmonic overtones (Source :Wikipedia).

Some of these beautiful bowls made of *ashtadhatu* are available in Lahaul and Spiti and also at Tibetan markets in various cities. These are few in number but the market is also flooded with modern industrial cast bowls which are not very expensive. Along with these, chimes, Tibetan gongs, bells and specialized tuning forks are also used for cleansing with sound. The cleansing frequency that works for most crystals and people is 528 Hz and 512 Hz. These can be accessed from YouTube as can a range of cleansing and energising sounds for all chakras. An i-phone app called chakra pro also promises to do the same.

The most important factor in using sound for cleansing crystals and spaces is intention. The exact frequency of your temple bell or singing bowl does not matter (though apps are available to measure their frequencies), only the intention to cleanse does matter. Sound healing is a fascinating new area of study. As usual everyone should abide by their own comfort level with any given sound: the intuition being our final guide.

(A word of caution. Certain trance music and some binaural beat audios can be addictive just like a drug for the brain. Tuning forks of specific frequency sounds played for a short period around the crystals is a better option than to get hooked on, with headphones for a long period, to unknown and potentially dangerous binaural beats videos.)

A *ghanti* or temple bell can work just as well.

Always the First: Clear Quartz

A very common question among first time crystal users is which one crystal one should begin with. In my opinion, Clear Quartz is the perfect stone, though some prefer Amethyst for beginning and supporting their spiritual journey. But then, Amethyst is also a quartz. Clear Quartz is inexpensive, accessible (especially in India) and easy to get used to.

Quartz is a silicate, a mixture of silicon and oxygen (Silicon di-oxide) and is one of the most commonly found crystals in the world. The variety of its forms and colours is mind-boggling. It spans a wide range from the clear sparkle of the hexagonal prismatic Clear Quartz, to other macro-crystalline forms like Pink Quartz and pink coloured Rose Quartz, violet Amethyst, dazzling blue quartzes both natural and manmade, yellow brown Citrines, brown Smoky Quartz, Ametrine, Agate, Aventurine , chatoyant Hawk's Eye, Tiger's Eye and Cat's Eye (lehsunia), and Rutilated Quartz. Its micro-crystalline forms include Agates, Carnelian, Chalcedony, Chrysopase and Onyx. Jasper is a grainy variety of Quartz. The list of various kinds of Quartz is very long and includes recent finds from Himalayas in areas where glaciers have receded (Nirvana Quartz, Anandalite, Pink or Samadhi Quartz though the reader need not invest in these more expensive varieties unless guided to do so).

Quartz is used in computers, microphones, radios, watches, ultrasound devices etc. because of its property of piezoelectricity: i.e. it can transform mechanical energy into electromagnetic energy and vice-versa. Quartz is a component of Granite, Quartzite, Mica and Sandstone. It is widely found in the Himalayas and has been used as Sphatik malas by Hindus for prayer and healing benefits. I feel some of the uplifting effect of being in the Himalayan regions comes from the large component of Quartz found in the rocks. It is quite possible that the palace of Maya described in the Sabha Parva of the *Mahabharata* had pond floors made of quartz which Duryodhana mistakes for water.

The Japanese refer to it as the perfect jewel and it has been revered in Burma, North America, South America, Europe and Australia. It is found in almost every part of the world. It is also an important part of glass. In short, we are surrounded by varied forms of quartz in our daily life.

However, it takes on a special power when we wear or keep a piece of Clear Quartz with a positive intention. Quartz stores, radiates, memorizes and amplifies energy. It is the most versatile and multipurpose stone and has been used traditionally to promote good health and peaceful sleep, to provide protection from negative energies and increase focus and memory. It can be used for any purpose if programmed with right intentions. It loves to be charged in the sunlight and needs to washed frequently (preferably with sea-salt and water) as it stores all kinds of energy. It is usually gentle and suitable for beginners though the reader must observe how they feel around it. Being an inexpensive and pretty stone, clusters of Quartz can be kept around the house to raise the energy levels. However, a person who is depressed or in a negative mood must exercise caution as Quartz basically amplifies one's own energy and vibration. It works in harmony with any other stone or crystal, often amplifying their effects. I see it primarily as an energy generator, a powerful gift of nature that gently assists our evolution and enhances our potential. It attunes us to our intuition and over a period of time increases our psychic gifts. It makes our aura wider and more attractive, hence usually helps in attracting people and opportunities that are right for us. It can help students and writers with the gift of clarity, focus and enhanced memory. It is used by healers worldwide including those who send Reiki.

In physical healing it is especially beneficial for balancing all systems, increasing immunity, regulating metabolism and helping one assess the cause of a disease. In terms of chakras, though it works to protect and balance the entire aura, it resonates especially with the Crown Chakra, bringing alignment with Higher Guidance and to help us see our purpose in life. It can protect sensitive people and empaths from energy drainage.

Above all, the greatness of this stone is that one can use affirmation and intention to make it do whatever one wants as long as it is for the higher good of oneself and others. That is of course, if one is willing to follow up (with purposeful action) on the self-knowledge and clarity that this stone brings. Because it is so sensitive to energy and intention it needs clearing constantly. Apart from salt and water, incense smoke, keeping it in the prayer area or periodically placing it in a flower pot (under soil) are some of the other methods to help cleanse it with focussed intention.

Transparent Clear Quartz spheres with rainbows radiate sheer joy and angelic guidance. Just looking at any quartz connects us to nature and fills the mind with wonder and gratitude to the Divine.

It is a super stone of protection, power, clarity, improved health and sheer spiritual bliss as long as one keeps one's intentions clear and focussed on the forces of Light rather than on any negative feelings of resentment, anger, depression, hatred and revenge. Used with prayer, faith and positive intentions, it is pure easy magic. Clear Quartz is a classic worth investing in.

Amber

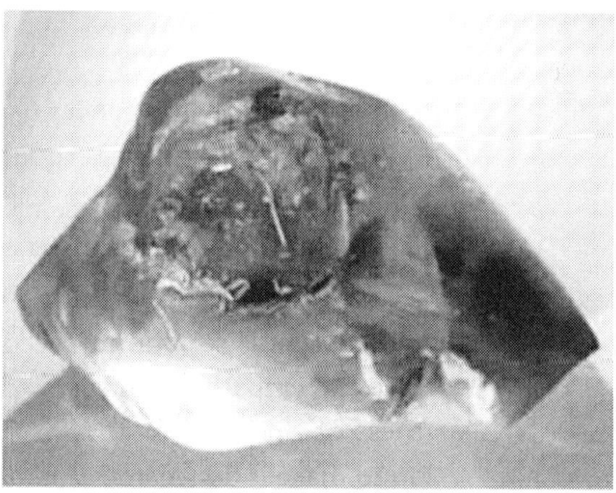

Throughout history Amber has been used as a healing and protective stone. Actually, it is not really a stone but resin that is millions of year old, has fossilized and often has plant or animal debris trapped in it. It ranges from clear to honey yellow to orangey brown and may be clear or opaque.

Scandinavian women would use amber spindles to spin protective garments for warrior husbands and sons. In the Orient, the stone was believed to inspire courage in the wearer. It was also used to cure headaches and heal wounds.

Amber is the stone for detoxification and clearing blockages. It is supposed to draw disease away from the body, especially if it is chronic and builds immunity. It is considered to be anti-bacterial and analgesic in nature. It is a gentle energiser and uplifting in its effects. It is soothing, especially for anxiety, and has a very beneficial effect on the nervous system. Its outer cortex is composed of succinic acid that is supposed to be a powerful antioxidant and helps in healing disruptions of cardiac rhythm. It also aids in the recovery of the neural system and enhances awareness and concentration.

Amber has traditionally been used to bring babies comfort during teething. It has also been used and is still used to bring pain relief in joints and tissues for patients of rheumatism and arthritis. It is also claimed to increase potency, help with the pain of childbirth and gall stone pain. In Russia it is promoted even today as a stone with anti- ageing and cell rejuvenating benefits.

In work situations it overcomes confrontational attitudes in others. It reduces confusion and promotes creative thinking and peacefulness. It also protects from electromagnetic radiation and it is good to keep it near cell phones and pcs.

It can be used in elixir form or worn as pretty jewellery. One website suggests this method to differentiate fake amber/plastic from real: take one part salt and two parts water and dissolve. Real amber will float on it. That is how it lands on Baltic shores as it is often found floating on saline sea water or entangled in sea weed.

Amber is truly an amazing creation of nature that protects, connects us to earth energy, heals and rejuvenates.

Amethyst

The absolutely amazing Amethyst has been known as a magical stone since ancient times. Its Hindi name is Kathela or Jamunia.

This master healer stone derives its name from the Greek word Amethystos, which means a (not) — methys (spirit or drink) i.e. not drunk or intoxicated. From the time the Greeks and Romans made amulets and talismans of Amethyst to dilute and reduce their wine intake, it has been used as a sobriety stone. Even today it is credited with helping de-addiction of many kinds: from alcohol, drugs, smoking as well as from destructive compulsive behaviours. It works with the crown and third eye chakras and is supposed to impact the pituitary and pineal glands. It also helps open the heart chakra.

Amethyst is crystalline quartz found in bewitchingly beautiful shades of purple, mauve, and lilac. It is a commonly available crystal and is seen in crystal shops in various forms including dark grape shaped intriguing inward looking geodes, inviting brilliant clusters, pyramids, spheres and in many pretty items of jewellery. The purple colouration comes from iron impurities, its formula being $Si\ O_2 + Fe$. It pales with exposure to sunlight and clusters especially must be kept in shade. Like Clear Quartz, Amethyst focuses and amplifies energy and is similarly used to make healing wands used to direct and deflect energy.

Amethyst is incredibly calming and has been used for aiding restful slumber. It may affect different users in different ways and some people who sleep with it under their pillow may wake up after six hours because it prevents oversleeping as well. In all cases however, it gives restful sleep, free from nightmares.

Amethyst's cousin Ametrine (amethyst + citrine) is also a powerful healer, relieving restlessness and anxiety. Both Amethyst and Ametrine bring clarity to thinking and aid memory. Ametrine helps with fluid metabolism, metabolic issues, auto-immune disorders and intestinal health.

Amethyst is supposed to accelerate spiritual growth, enhance visions and intuition in general. It is a favoured stone for meditation. Amethyst brings up deeply held restrictive beliefs for the purpose of self-transformation. Sue and Simon Lily class it as a violet stone combining the grounding energy of red with the expansive psychic flights of blue and indigo stones, hence as an effective balancing stone for the whole aura.

In healing it is supposed to be one of the most effective stones for regulating the endocrine and immune systems and beneficial for the circulatory and digestive systems. It is credited with helping fight tumours, assisting in healing arthritis, diabetes, fibromyalgia, chronic fatigue, headaches, insomnia, lung problems, asthma; in easing PMS and menopause; in regulating intestinal flora and absorption: the list compiled from various sources runs very long indeed. It helps with psychological as well as geopathic stress. Amethyst kept in a room is a like a psychic air –purifier bringing in calm and positivity. However, some people report it to be extremely energising.

Amethyst has also always been used for psychic protection and protection from thieves while travelling. It is also employed as a pain reliever. As always, one must use individual intuition to judge the suitability of and comfort level with a crystal. Overall, amethyst and clear quartz qualify as all round healers combining beauty, power and protection.

Angelite

Azure Angelite is a calmness inducing stone and like most blue stones, it is a great facilitator of correct communication.

The colour of a clear sky and its serenity is reflected in tumbled Angelite; in its raw form it usually displays shades of grey, blue and white. Also called anhydrite (which means without water), it is a calcium sulphate mineral that has been discovered fairly recently in Peru.– It is fragile and should not be washed in water as it may dissolve to form gypsum. Angelite is formed from Celestitewhich has been compressed for a million years and shares many properties with the same crystal.

Angelite helps us deal with anger against oneself or others. It assists us to say the right thing at the right moment. It is predominantly a throat chakra stone that helps with thyroid and communication related issues. It instils sound sleep as well as lucid dream recall. It is protective during sleep and meditation. It offers general protection from entities and negative energy.

Angelite is credited with telepathic qualities in that some believe that two people who want to be in touch psychically when apart can both keep a piece of Angelite with them (and program it with this intent).

Angelite helps recovery from past abuse and hurt and is especially helpful to healers and anyone who wants to enhance their psychic perceptions. Most crystals (eg. Lapis lazuli,Clear Quartz, Amethyst, Selenite, to name just a few) do this but different people prefer different stones for their spiritual evolution. It depends on which crystal "calls" you.

Apart from the throat and thyroid, Angelite works like magic on the circulatory system. It helps with haemoglobin related disorders.Angelite aids detoxification and speeds healing from infections.It also helps increase the range of motion in joints and is thus useful for arthritis patients, who have reported the dual benefit of peaceful sleep during a painful episode when sleeping with Angelite. However, every person reacts differently to stones and thus, individual discretion and observation is advised. No crystal should replace existing medication.Angelite has also been recommended for weight lossand diabetics as it leads to a balanced approach which encourages healthy eating.

This new age stone is believed to connect one to one's higher self and one's guides and angels and can be used in conjunction with Seraphinite or Danburite also. It is believed to provide protection during meditation, out of body experiences and astral travel, for which purpose it can be combined with Moldavite: that powerful tektite. If used thus it must be combined with a grounding and protective stone such as Nuumite or Hematite or black Tourmaline. It helps in connecting with one's guide or higher intelligence.Sometimes issues may be brought up for clearing (in a gentle way) so that one can deal with them. These could be any hidden fears or discontent holding us back.

A rebirthing and healing crystal, tranquil Angelite is great for new beginnings and for feeling calm, collected and in control.

Apatite

Free will is exerted in manifesting and Apatite is a crystal that helps manifestation. Whether the goal be as mundane as weight loss or profound as in enhancing psychic perception and opening up one's consciousness, whether it be materialistic as in manifesting abundance or devoting oneself to environmental activism, organic farming or altruism of any kind: Apatite has been credited with assisting with bringing one closer to desired outcomes.

Michael Gienger says that Apatite helps with apathy. It encourages liveliness and helps with exhaustion. It helps us find a balance between extreme activity and inertia and is claimed to be beneficial for autistic and hyperactive children. It calms aggression and irritability.

The word Apatite comes from the Greek word meaning "to deceive" as its various colours cause it to be confused with many other minerals. The name is ironic because Apatite actually puts us in touch with ourselves. It is a calcium phosphate mineral that can be yellow, blue, green, grey, colourless or a mix of two colours.

Blue Apatite is linked to the throat and third eye chakra and associated with enhancing psychic ability and group communication. It improves inner vision and the ability to learn from dreams. It has an uplifting and hopeful energy.

Yellow or Golden Apatite is termed as "one of the purest crystals of the yellow Ray" by Robert Simmons, who links it to "the vibration of mental clarity, strength of will and manifestation." (*The Book of Stones, 43).* This manifestation can be of prosperity and increased courage and charisma. He cautions that someone who is already overconfident might become too assertive for others' liking if they wear golden apatite. It is good for business people, sportspeople and anyone who needs to develop their will power in a competitive environment. This Apatite is associated with the solar plexus which is the seat of self-esteem and will power. It is also the chakra associated with digestion and though all Apatites assist weight loss, probably green and yellow ones do it the best. This is achieved through hunger suppression that this stone is credited with but also because of its positive effect on metabolism and energy levels. Needless to say, a crystal can just aid lifestyle changes, helping us in our journey of making sensible eating choices and exercising regularly and not replace our own agency or volition. That said, it is true that Apatite can help make exercise more effective. For weight management goals this crystal can be combined with Amethyst (to fight addictions), with Citrine (for digestion, sunny disposition and motivation), with Calcite or Fluorite for clear sighted goals and methodical progress, with Sodalite (for metabolism especially regulation of fluids), Amber, Quartz etc. One's intuition is the best guide. However, crystals cannot replace regular medication especially when a person has been diagnosed with a metabolic or hormonal disorder. And yet, together with the help of intent, crystals and sound medical guidance one can progress towards improved health and fitness.

Apatite is also a healer of bones and joints (its phosphorous content allies it with the skeletal system) and helps in the absorption of calcium. It balances underactive as well as overactive chakras. GreenApatite, the heart chakra stone is a great stress reliever and is beneficial for the heart. It helps with communication, social networking and environmental issues. Apatite used with other stones enhances their effect. This might be because of its reputed ability to speed up results.

Apatite can help us make new friends and renew our zest for life. Eason calls it the "bones of earth" and a premier earth and natural healing stone (*The New Crystal Bible*, 251).

Apatite inspires us to hope and to develop the motivation and the drive to manifest the life we want on all levels: physical, material, natural, emotional, spiritual. It is simultaneously mysterious and otherworldly as well as being pragmatic as it urges us to move ahead with positive changes.

Apophyllite

A hydrated potassium calcium silicate mineral, Apophyllite is a master healer. It is abundant in white and colourless varieties mostly but grey and green are also found and valued. It is easily available in India, especially in Poona and Nasik and also found in some European and South American countries.

A cluster of Apophyllite can be appropriately placed in a space for clearing and cleansing. This is primarily a crown chakra stone though the green one works on the heart chakra as well. It is great for meditation, channelling and healing especially remote healing. It is also known as the Reiki stone as it supplements Reiki and has the same gentle energy though it is fast acting. Some clusters contain Stillbite as well (embedded in the Apophyllite matrix). Both together assist in soul journeys, astral travel and are protective of the brain. Both reveal occult information though Stillbite has a more passive and hermit like energy. Apophyllite is used more for meditation and making contact with one's guides than for healing physical ailments. It can however, be used as a medium for sending Reiki and other kinds of overall healing. It has a positive impact on mental health issues especially on paranoia and schizophrenia.

It raises one's frequency and keeps away negativity. It aids in getting rid of harmful habits and company. It is useful for respiratory issues especially allergies and asthma. It can help the body with absorption of certain minerals like potassium and magnesium and also with certain vitamins. Green Apophyllite can improve one's connection with nature, animals and plants. Cassandra Eason calls Apophyllite a horse whisperer stone and claims that it helps communication with horses. It is a stone of detoxification and renewed innocence. It is very healing for emotional stress.

Apophyllite reveals its powers to those who meditate with it and explore its healing potential. It is a crystal that puts us in touch with other realms and worlds. An energy healer can use it as a wand to remove cords, regenerate tissues and raise one's vibrational frequency. Apophyllite has an angelic energy and is a protective and calming stone to have around.

Aquamarine

The name Aquamarine means "water of the sea" and both sky and water are evoked by this blue and blue-green stone. Tumbled Himalayan aquamarine is somewhat more glassy greenish recalling the grace of mighty mountain rivers like the Ganges. It is a beryl, a beryllium aluminium silicate mineral. It was (and still is) believed to offer protection to sailors, to swimmers and all those travelling over water.

It is widely acknowledged to be one of the strongest stones for the throat chakra, facilitating communication at all levels. It assists both speaking out and singing clearly. It is a stone of courage that helps reveal old patterns that may keep us stuck and gives a quiet courage to release those patterns and start new projects and develop new perspectives. It helps children who have faced or those who fear verbal abuse and negativity. It calms similar fears and anxieties in adults especially if the issues involved go back to childhood trauma of any kind.

It is a cooling and anti-inflammatory stone which is especially effective for inflammation in the nasal area, upper respiratory tract and the food pipe. It can help manage food intolerances and benefits the ovaries and kidneys as well. Like Apatite it can be programmed for appetite regulation and to develop sensible eating habits. It enhances immunity. It is a very good stone for thyroid health. It has a light-hearted energy and people with lots of negativity to work through may not be attracted to it. It brings back a quiet joy and helps recover radical innocence within oneself.

Aventurine

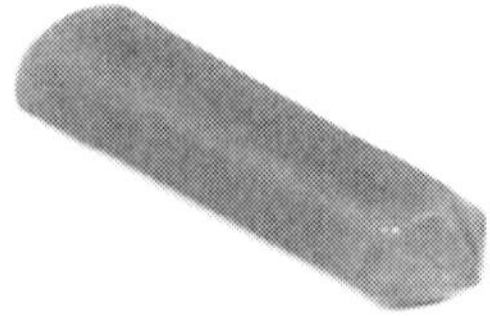

Go green with Aventurine ! Not only is soft green the most easily available colour in this crystal, which is also found in blue, red, brown and peach colours, but it is also used to grid gardens as it protects plants from geopathic stress (i.e. "stress created by subtle emanations and energy disturbances from underground water, power lines and negative earth energy lines"-Judy Hall). It also protects us from electromagnetic emanations.

Like all green stones, it resonates with the heart centre. Like Peridot it calms resentment, anger and irritability, but Aventurine is much gentler in its operations. If one places a crystal like Malachite on the heart center, or Lapiz on the third eye, or Peridot or Rhodochrosite on the solar plexus, or if one works with Obsidian; all of these strong crystals bring up repressed issues at once(to one's consciousness), which then can be dissolved by using Aventurine with any of them. By itself too, it is a great balancer of the heart chakra and helps in overall healing, revealing the source of the disease in the past. It has a very calming presence and can reduce conflicts when placed in work spaces, or home. It is often used in healing wands used during energy healing practices. It can complement the healing process in patients recovering from heart surgery and high blood pressure.

It is said to help with stammering, neurosis, nausea, joint stiffness, sciatica and low –back pain in general. For back pain it can be placed on the site of pain, though of course, this is not a substitute for a medical consultation. Aventurine wands can be used for energy healing.

Aventurine is considered to be a good-luck stone, possibly because it removes blocks to attracting abundance. Since it diffuses harsh energies it can be kept in healing rooms, conference rooms, lobbies at homes and hotels and spas.This tranquil stone is also protective of its wearer's heart energy, preventing it from being drained by others.

Calcite

In a recent study, the material most suitable to make an invisibility cloak (the kind that Harry Potter wears), is Clear Calcite. If you draw a line and view it through a clear calcite crystal: it appears double. It is believed in folklore, that calcite was used to double the power of spells. It is indeed a great amplifier of energy and good for students, for it encourages clarity of thought. Clarity helps in relationships as well, and calcite is a great balancer of emotions. Paradoxically, can also help one keep a low profile and not seem very visible when the wearer needs to do so.

Clear calcite or Iceland Spar is the stable form of calcium carbonate. All calcites have a high calcium content are very strengthening for the bones. The presence of other minerals leads to the formation of the other pretty colours, such as red, mangano pink, honey, orange, green, blue, violet and white calcites respectively. Each of these calcites relates to the corresponding chakra of its colour eg. Orange calcite relates to the sacral chakra and works on the female reproductive system and bowel related disorders. It helps in nutrient assimilation especially of calcium, and relationship issues especially those tinged with anxiety and fear. Orange calcite also helps in balancing sexual energy. Like clear calcite, it is a great mover of energy and helps come up with clear solutions, both in personal and professional life. It can help one access the joy within oneself.

Clear Calcite is connected to the crown and third eye chakra though it is supposed to clear imbalances when placed on any of the chakra points. Meditating with calcite can be an enchanting experience if it is indeed your stone. One can gaze at the striations within that sometimes seem to shift shape. It is believed that meditating with it or simply gazing at it can help us come closer to understand our purpose in the world. One of the most fascinating finds in this dual refractive stone is a calcite with a rainbow in it. It is supposed to bring new beginnings into one's life and is a joy to gaze at.

Being an overall grounding, centring and balancing stone, it is emotionally very healing, and also helps in reading double meanings, thus cutting through confusion. It brings hope. Physically, it is a cleansing and detoxifying stone. It is healing for back pain, and ailments affecting eyes and teeth. Its elixir works on a wide range of conditions, including those of the skin, like warts and ulcers. Athletes can use it to increase bone strength and students, to boost memory.

It can be cleaned under running water and charged in moonlight, or by keeping it on a clear quartz cluster. Considered sacred by the Native Americans once, Calcite is readily available today, and can be used as an aid to energise our bodies, and to balance our emotions with our intellect. It can also raise our consciousness overall, if it chooses to reveal its magic to us!

Carnelian

Athletes could use this crystal as a pick me up, so energising is its effect.

A pretty orange crystal, easily available and used extensively in silver jewellery in India, Carnelian is also found in pink, red and brown colours. In fact, the best Carnelian is found in India. Carnelian is a crystal that revitalizes the body and stimulates creativity. For long it has been associated with qualities of leadership and courage. It is a great stone for new beginnings and decision making. It helps one stop procrastinating and believing in oneself enough to take instant action. It can be used to cleanse other stones. It is a protective stone and was used in ancient times for protection and shielding against enchantment and negativity. On the emotional level, it helps recovery from abuse of any kind. It protects from anger and resentment from within and without.

It is said to work on many chakras: base (especially red carnelian), sacral (stimulates sexual energy and increases fertility, heals testes and ovaries), solar as well as heart chakras (especially, pink carnelian). In healing it is especially useful in:

- Relieving pain, especially back pain and any pain caused by anxiety. However, this may vary among individuals.
- Aids absorption of nutrients and it is believed that meditating with it can alert one to any food allergies and intolerances
- Helps regulate fluids and stimulates metabolism
- Recommended for nose bleeds
- Boosts energy levels
- Beneficial in menstrual cramps and boosts fertility.

Keeping Carnelian near one's study area can increase concentration. It is an overall grounding stone, which guides us about out our orientation in the present and alerts us to any future pitfalls and roadblocks in the directions we are following at the moment. It removes emotions that are not good for us and shows us which relationships or issues are distracting us from achieving our goals. It can also be used if one wants to keep one's thoughts private and not have one read easily by others.

Most people find it a comforting and joyous stone, much like Sun-stone, but in case it feels too overwhelming, or energising, one can wear a blue or green stone along with it. "Feeling" a stone's energy is very individual and one's own intuition should be the final guide. If you feel attracted to it, you probably need it.

Celestite

Celestite is instantly identifiable by its sky blue pyramidal crystals though it may also be found in red, white and yellow shades. It draws you into its glistening depths, and transports one to a

place of utter calm and deep peace. To me it seems most like a Himalayan glacier, the ice crystals melting into pure water, pure higher consciousness.

The very name of this crystal suggests the celestial realm, as does its other, earlier name Celestine. It is one of the favourite stones, of energy workers and those who use crystals to aid meditation. A geode or a cluster of Celestite kept in any room brings an instant sense of harmony in a group, and of de-cluttering the individual mind of repetitive worries. It is an excellent stone for the mind, helping in studies by increasing rationality and enhancing the ability to picture information, in order to better access and express it. This makes it useful for students, artists, writer s, and those pursuing graphic design. Like all light blue stones it resonates with the throat chakra, which makes it excellent for speakers, teachers, and singers as well.

Along with the rational faculties of the mind, it paradoxically, also jumpstarts intuition and works on the crown chakra. It is also believed that meditating by placing it on the third eye gives very interesting results. It is a new age stone with a very high vibration, one which is said to hold ancient wisdom and facilitate angel communication and clairaudient communication with higher dimensions.

In healing, it is specifically used for disorders of the eye and ear. It is an overall balancing crystal for all the chakras and emotional and spiritual wellbeing. It also benefits the intestines and the colon. This fragile crystal should be kept away from sunlight as it loses its colour easily. The best ones come from Madagascar and can be a bit expensive. Bring home this ethereal crystal to surround yourself with its incredible peace, to unravel the depths of the mind and to meditate.

Chrysocolla

It looks quite a bit like turquoise and is in fact, found quite often mixed with it or azurite or malachite. This soothing blue – green stone is said to have been carried everywhere by the Egyptian Queen Cleopatra, because of its ability to resolve conflicts in groups, and calm frayed tempers, thus making it useful for diplomatic negotiation. Found wherever large deposits of copper abound, as for example in Mexico, Africa and Arizona, it is composed of copper silicate. It has been revered for its healing properties in diverse cultures such as Native American shamanism, Egyptian and African legends, and Tibetan, to name a few.

Chrysocolla is good for overall balancing of chakras though it is specifically associated with the fifth(throat) chakra and communication. This crystal calms , cleanses and reenergises all chakras. It can uncover sexual issues for healing bringing to light destructive patterns that repeat themselves in relationships. It highlights blocks in communication and helps improve communication at all levels. It removes blocks to abundance and creative expression as well. It gives the confidence to re-examine long held beliefs.

It is known especially for its healing benefits for lungs, and assists the healing of CFS (chronic fatigue syndrome), which brings down the efficiency of the functioning of vital organs like the lungs. Chrysocolla also works on the pancreas and helps insulin metabolism, thus making it useful for diabetics and those who are insulin resistant. It is one of the crystals used for a range of new lifestyle diseases, which conventional medicine cannot fully account for or cure (CFS, fibromyalgia, IBS, adrenal fatigue etc), with this important disclaimer, however: crystals are to be used to complement, and not replace a medical healthcare regimen and healthy life-style choices. Chrysocolla relieves arthritic pain, lowers blood pressure, strengthens thyroid and is very good for the overall metabolism of the body.

Most importantly, Chrysocolla healing takes place on an emotional level. It will not bring emotions to the surface, in a way that lapis, azurite, malachite, obsidian, quartz especially smoky quartz quickly can, but it helps resolve any emotional turmoil that has surfaced. Guilt, resentment, long held grief, hurt especially caused by a loved one, abuse within family: these are some of the issues that we can let go by holding this crystal or gazing into its multihued depths. It opens the heart to unconditional love. It helps with PMS and menstrual cramps which is in keeping with its energy that has been perceived as feminine. Very gently, it brings harmony in the house or work and study area, enhancing creative communication and tolerance, releasing guilt and bringing a quiet joy.

Citrine

Citrine is the crystal of knowledge, abundance and generosity: all Jupiterian impulses.

One of the birthstones for those born in November, golden yellow Citrine(SiO_2) is a joy to look at, and that is what it brings to the wearer, among other gifts. Crystals may range from clear lemon yellow to orange and brown with white areas. Most Citrine these days is made by subjecting low quality amethyst to slow heat. Irrespective of its origin, different shades of Citrine have healing properties. The brown in it helps in grounding, the orange balances the sacral chakra and the yellows strengthen the solar chakra: thus providing confidence (base chakra and solar) as well as enhancing creative thinking (sacral). It is quite versatile depending on the colour and composition of the individual pieces. The orange brown ones can help remove writer's block, the yellow ones inspire clear thinking and most Citrine is very good for taking decisions about managing finances and attracting people to shops. It is a good luck stone with a tendency to create serendipity.

Citrine is a perennial favourite with energy workers, because apart from Kyanite, it is thought to be the only other stone to never hold negativity and hence, it never needs cleaning. However, I think all crystals benefit from clearing their energy periodically. Citrine is believed to cleanse negative energy, dissolve and transform it and ground any excess. It protects from abuse and energy drain. It is also valued as an energy generator.

Citrine is useful for students and all others who are anxious when brainstorming. Citrine calms anxiety and nervousness, especially the clear yellow varieties, and aids clear thinking. Simultaneously, it helps heal digestive disorders because often indigestion is a physical manifestation of an inability to digest and assimilate new ideas or an inability to cope with change.

In crystal shops the sales person assures you that Citrine in the cash box multiplies sales and money. Many keep it in the wealth corner of the house. However, Citrine also encourages sharing your abundance, a lesson that came home to me when I realized I kept gifting away all Citrines I owned to those who I thought needed it!

In healing, Citrine as an energising stone is highly beneficial for CFS (Chronic Fatigue Syndrome).It stimulates the spleen, gall bladder, pancreas and the liver, aiding digestion overall. It also works on infections of bladder and kidney. Judy Hall also highlights its role in balancing the thymus and thyroid, increasing blood circulation and helping with eye problems as well as menstrual ones. Of course crystals must be used to supplement and not replace any existing medical regimens. Wear it or keep it or share it: this is a stone that carries the power of the sun and imparts energy, joy and abundance.

Crystals for Moving On

The title of this article can be misleading as crystals, however wonderful their properties might be, cannot by themselves help us move on: unless we really want to do so. Crystals work with intention and support and supplement other healing and self-transforming programmes we may set for ourselves. That said, they are our powerful allies in the painful process of moving on.

Nobody likes change except a wet baby. Change, when we do not willingly adopt it, is thrust on us for our progress and higher good. Patterns of behaviour that no longer serve us need to be dropped and dysfunctional relationships come to an end once they have served their purpose. Often our energy may be so entangled with another's that even after a formal break up, we might find ourselves unable to escape the lingering emotional pain of longing, of what ifs and sometimes of resentment. If the relationship was an abusive one, the partner might have left energy hooks that hinder the moving on process. The best way to start with the process in such cases would be to cut energy ties binding one to a former friend or partner. The visualizing of cutting psychic cords is harmless (to both the persons involved) and results in severing of destructive and draining emotional ties.

The next thing to do is to calmly meditate or introspect on one's own life and identify destructive patterns that have structured our lives and will go on repeating themselves till we learn the lesson and truly move on. For example if X attracts men who always take advantage of her, and leave when she needs commitment or support, then X needs to take cognisance of this pattern and trace it to childhood relationships with her parents: perhaps her father was emotionally distant and she learnt to fix things for others early on in life to earn approval. She now continues the pattern in a series of failed relationships. She needs to change her energy first by reclaiming her power and learning to be happy as a single before she jumps into yet another relationship. Or Y 's mother was emotionally unavailable for him in childhood which makes him distrust women and run from emotional intimacy.

Crystals can help with this necessary but not always pleasant process of self-knowledge. The choice of crystals depends on where the energy blockages are affecting a person. An energy healing modality like Reiki or Pranic Healing can help further in becoming sensitive in this respect. However, for most people, the biggest clue is their gut feeling when they see and hold a crystal in a store or elsewhere. What attracts you is what you need. This could be pink stones like Pink Quartz and Rhodochrosite to calm the heart and love oneself unconditionally. It could be a Malachite or Lapis lazuli that will bring all repressed emotions to surface in a crying bout, which can then be dissolved with a Unakite, Rhodochrosite or Peridot. Rhodochrocite will help one breathe deeply, and Unakite can be used to breathe out and release those painful feelings. Peridot is also good for hidden resentment or anger directed at self or the other. Stones with a high lithium content, like Lepidolite, Lepidochrosite, Pink Tourmaline and Sugilite can bring relief in depression and alleviate insomnia brought about by emotional stress. Lithium calms the nerves and is an effective antidepressant. Lepidolite also helps one stand in one's own space. Tiger's eye, Carnelian and Clear Quartz are protective of the aura and Tiger's eye, as well, as Sunstone help in cutting energy hooks. Clear Quartz can help dissolve blockages anywhere rapidly. Tiger's Eye and Sunstone two stones also act upon the sacral chakra, the area where we tend to cling on to emotions and pain. Solar plexus the seat of our self esteem and identity is helped with yellow stones like Tiger's eye and Citrine as well as green stones like Unakite. If unsure what to use, always go with Clear Quartz, which will act in accordance with the intention set by the wearer. Calcite, Quartz and Fluorites are good for new beginnings, diverting the mind to things to be accomplished. Chrysocolla is calming and healing, Turquoise diverting and joyous, Amethyst, Amazonite, Aventurine are all heart healing and Quartz, Apophyllite, Labradorite and Amethyst link us to our higher spiritual purpose.

Different stones might be needed in different phases of moving on. If any stone makes one uncomfortable or sad or oversensitive or restless, it must be set aside. Trust your intuition and develop a positive attitude to change. One must actively work towards eliminating co-dependency, trying to identify destructive patterns in relationships that might otherwise keep playing out in future associations. Crystals can help with both.

Fluorite

Fluorite is credited with "balancing brain chemistry" by Naisha Ahsian. It seems that Green fluorite goes a step further and balances the decisions of the mind with the heart and helps us harmonize with nature. Most crystal experts see fluorite as a psychic vacuum cleaner, collecting all doubts, negativity and mental clutter into a heap, getting rid of it and stimulating the mind to take creative decisions with clarity and also to structure

one's energy and assignments.

The name Flourite derives from the Latin word "Fleure", which means: 'to flow', which denotes "additives that enable an ore to reach melting point more quickly" (Micheal Gienger, *Crystal Power Crystal Healing,* 284). Composed of Calcium Fluoride, it is used as a source of fluorine for fluorinated water. It is associated with fluoride which prevents tooth decay. Fluorite was known as fluorspar, since the eighteenth century. A spar is a mineral that breaks into leaves. Quite a few specimens of fluoride display fluorescence under UV light: they glow in the dark. But apart from these obvious physical properties, many metaphysical properties are attributed to this "Genius Stone", which is another name for fluorite. Its octahedron structure, composed of two fused pyramidal shapes, is said to give it a "sacred geometry". Fluorite brings order and structure at every level, including the cellular level in an organism.

There would be two advantages of keeping it on one's study table or work area: It helps in learning, organizing and sorting ideas; and it has an amazing ability to absorb computer and electromagnetic emanations. When kept near a computer, it will absorb negative energies and stress, along with any electromagnetic radiation from the surroundings. It is also an immense healer overall: gently protective of the aura as it stabilizes and balances it. Used for either of these purposes, i.e. cleansing the surroundings or healing the person, fluorite should be cleansed in running water regularly, but carefully, because it is a soft stone. After cleansing, it must be charged in sunlight or moonlight.

Fluorite is associated with the third eye, throat and heart chakras, with specially its purple variety responding to the mind(brow) and mental-spiritual issues, blue fluorite with communication (throat) and especially with psychic communication; green fluorite with balancing and healing the heart. Yellow fluorite is associated more with creativity and group work, healing the organs associated with the solar plexus centre and also helps people deal with competition.It can help with regulating the liver, kidneys and spleen and is said to help with cholesterol mechanism.

Green fluorite is associated strongly with the healing of stomach and intestines, and is especially useful for reducing the pain of stomach cramps. Gazing into the depths of a piece of the beautifully striated green fluorite, is like looking at the heart of the ocean, and the calm that it brings to the feelings is similar, which is why it is such a good healer for emotional traumas, and an aura cleanser, especially good for self-healing. It helps bring subconscious feelings to surface, and encourages acceptance of new ideas and circumstances.

Blue fluorite is very good for throat infections, healing the ears, nose, and throat. Purple and blue varieties, also pink and magenta are all associated with developing the intuition. Purple fluorite in particular is supposed to promote spiritual vision and aid in developing discrimination. Pink fluorite is used to reduce the pain and inflammation of spinal injuries, by certain practitioners.Clear transparent fluorite promotes spiritual harmony and is associated with the mystical properties of the crown chakra. Pretty rainbow fluorite is supposed to bring joy, creativity and have positive effects on the nervous system.it is calming and reassuring for fear and anxiety.

All Fluorite is believed to be useful for arthritis and helps ease stiffness in the back.It is highly beneficial for all the organs and secretions involved in digestion (especially the liver), female reproductive organs, inflammation and tumours.It is useful for soothing sore throats and reducing inflammation in the respiratory and digestive tracts. It helps manageasthma, and can protect arteries from fat deposits, regulating cholesterol and strengthening bones.Fluorite is useful for gum strength, and can assist with dental treatment (though it is certainly not a replacement for it!). It enhances the functioning of immune system and promotes cellular regeneration. It works on all these systems perhaps because it resolves unprocessed emotions and anger, helping reveal hidden causes of emotional disturbances.

It is an excellent learning aid and is useful for increasing concentration. Rainbow Fluorite which is multi-coloured balances thought with emotion and removes blocks anywhere in the body especially in the heart. It helps with practical execution of (creative) projects. All Fluorite provides structure to ideas and helps the wearer define boundaries better resulting in better management of time, energy and ideas.

Banishing chaos and bringing in balance, at the physical, auric and psychic levels, the benefits of fluorite are manifold and still revealing themselves.

Howlite

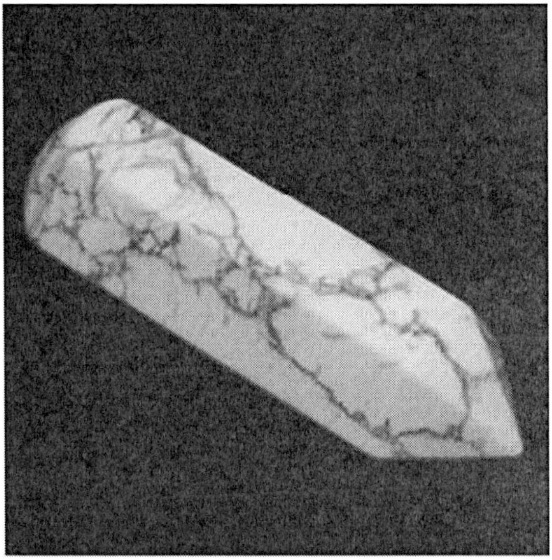

An extremely calming stone, Howlite (calcium boron- silicate hydroxide) was named after its discoverer Henry How, a geologist. It is easily obtained and inexpensive so it has the dubious distinction of being used as an imitation stone, especially as turquoise, when it is dyed blue.

Howlite is usually found in white with a web like pattern of grey or black veins. Howlite can be used in crowded places to generate patience. It can be used around argumentative people to produce all round calm for all parties present. It is useful in healing as it alleviates frustration and anger, especially in physical conditions where people feel helpless. Its white colour makes it a crown chakra stone, that helps resolve repressed anger through meditation. It has been reported to aid meditation practices and is also associated with the third chakra.

Howlite aids calcium absorption and is very healing for teeth, bones and soft tissues. It is helpful for joint pain and arthritis. It cures insomnia and can be used to grid around the bed. It is said to accelerate metabolism and heal skin conditions.

Emotionally, it promotes a positive outlook on life bringing clarity on issues and a calm perspective. An interesting use reported by Cassandra Eason is to place it in the garden to protect it from being dug up by moles or other predators! Howlite is an effective all round psychic diffuser, which helps replace anger and pain with positivity and the strength to go on.

Iolite

Beautiful blue Iolite derives its name from the Greek word "ion" which means violet, but it can vary in colour: appearing gray or yellow or displaying various shades of blue-violet, depending on its cut. This happens because of a property called pleochroism, which produces different colours in different directions of the crystal. It was because of this property that Iolite was used as a polarizing filter by Viking navigators who used it to look at the sun and determine direction, when lost while sailing the Atlantic Ocean. It also aids vision in the metaphysical sense, like most blue stones associated with the brow chakra, even as it is used popularly in jewellery because of its affordability. In Hindi, it is called Neeli. Apart from being the stone of psychic awareness, some of the recorded uses of Iolite are:

- It helps bring order in a chaotic life, encouraging good management of time, space and money. It is said to help overcome or successfully manage debts.
- It helps in concentration.
- It helps with sibling rivalry and family discord, encouraging feelings of security. Alternatively, if one's family has too many expectations, it can help a person determine what they really want to do.
- It is considered a good luck stone for travellers especially for those returning home.
- A sobriety stone, it helps overcome addictions and aids detoxification at all levels.
- Enhances creativity as well as vision (It was a popular Shamanic stone).
- Helps stay in the moment and that that aids meditation as well.
- Physically, it has been found effective to heal headaches, especially migraines and Meniere's disease. It is also useful for eyes. It is said to help cut fatty deposits in the body especially and in bringing down cholesterol levels. Interestingly, it was used in malaria afflicted zones in the past because of its reputed ability to ward off malaria. It is also beneficial for the pituitary and the respiratory system.

People's experiences with crystals vary and this holds true of Iolite as well which can bestow variously: a connection with one's inner voice and psychic awareness, flights into creativity or clarity of purpose and practical management skills. Personally, when I'm near my piece of raw grey-violet Iolite, it brings up memories which come up for clearing and resolving, perhaps from sub-conscious depths of the mind. The stone has also been credited with bringing up past life memories. It can make one more objective and help focus the mind on the work at hand, away from distracting emotions. It is especially useful for artists, poets, singers, teachers and writers.

A soft and gentle stone overall, Iolite helps resolve the past, come to terms with the present and help bring in the new with a fresh perspective.

Kyanite : Mover of Energy

The Greek word "Kyanos" or kuanos means deep blue, and that is the most common colour of the crystal Kyanite, which has a distinctive texture of bladed striations. The blue may be mixed with green, indigo, brown or black. In addition, Kyanite is found in other colours like pink, grey, white, yellow and orange. An aluminium silicate mineral, it has industrial applications because of its heat resistance. In the metaphysical world it is a crystal hero because Kyanite and Citrine are two crystals that are believed never to need cleansing because they do not accumulate negativity, though I think all crystals can do with periodic cleansing.

Kyanite comes across as a soothing and relaxing crystal and it may work in this manner for most people and situations. Kyanite and Sunstone are referred to as "happy" crystals. However, I have found that Kyanite is an extremely powerful crystal and worn as a pendant, can bring emotional issues to surface for clearing, sometimes a bit too quickly. Healers have sometimes used it to make a client express repressed grief and people who may not have cried for many years may be able to do so as part of a Kyanite aided healing process. When used for this purpose the Kyanite can be smudged with incense or cleansed with sound (as with a Tibetan bowl/gong) to clear it of residual emotions before re-use. Though a powerful healer for physical ailments, Kyanite works primarily to promote truth telling and communication (throat chakra), clarify emotions (heart chakra) and to heal psychological issues. Kyanite can ease communication and networking between people of different backgrounds. It dissolves energy blocks and generates new perspectives.

A lot of people use it for enhancing their meditation experience (third eye) and for spiritual development (crown). Some use it for enhancing dream recall in order to initiate healing through dream analysis. It is recommended highly for aligning chakras as well as for beginning meditation practice, as well as for protection from negativity. It is supposed to help instil confidence to face challenging situations and for truthful communication. It balances masculine and feminine energies. The ease with which one responds or reacts to a crystal varies among individuals and hence one's intuition is the best guide.

Among physical ailments that Kyanite assists in healing, Judy Hall lists muscular disorders, fevers, problems in the urogenital system, adrenals, obesity, thyroid issues and throat problems.

Cassandra Eason mentions its ability to promote mobility, cellular healing, voice and speech mobility improvement and removing constrictions anywhere in the body. Crystals, of course, are meant to supplement other prescribed healing and not to replace it.

Beautiful blue or grounding black: in any colour Kyanite packs a punch. It stimulates, protects, releases guilt, inspires dreams, aligns chakras and can make you light and happy: but it just might make you cry first.

Labradorite: The Stone of Transformation and Possibilities

Labradorite is a variety of feldspar that looks unassumingly dull and grey, till light hits the inclusions of magnetite crystals in it. This crystal displays an interesting property called labradorescence. When viewed from a particular angle, a Schiller effect is observed, i.e. a colourful play of light across cleavage planes and sliced layered sections, in colors that range from shimmering violets, peacock blues, greens and yellows, in varied combinations. This makes it a crystal that helps us shift our perspective, and hence our awareness. The multiple colours also make for different possibilities in energy healing. It helps clear negative energy also.

Labradorite is often called an enchanted stone. It helps one steer through periods of transformation and is highly protective of the aura. It prevents energy leaks from the auric field, in any kind of relationships with other people. It is a good stone to wear when one is feeling emotionally overwhelmed. Labradorite is said to enhance psychic abilities, especially when used with other brow chakra stones like Lapis lazuli and Shattuckite. It brings hidden issues to surface, including feelings and memories from the sub-conscious mind (and sometimes from alternate lives). Like any multi-coloured stone, it resonates with more than one chakra, and can therefore be worn at the ears (for clairaudience), higher heart chakra, or used in meditation at the third eye or be programmed for use with the crown and higher chakras. It can be used with many other stones like Moonstone, Sunstone, Pietersite, Magnesite, as well as its own sister variety, which is Yellow Labradorite, a stone used for channelling.

It is protective against psychic attacks and ill intentions of others. It cleanses the aura of psychic debris. It helps process change and makes one less fearful of it.

Apart from these esoteric properties reported by various users, Labradorite comes in useful for emotional and physical healing. It regulates metabolism, improves digestion and eases menstrual tensions. It is also useful in dealing with gout and rheumatism. It lowers blood pressure, perhaps because it lowers stress and anxiety. It helps heal disorders of vision. It is beneficial for the Urino- Genital system and adrenal health. Yellow Labradorite in particular heals the urinary system, intestines and colon. It protects against parasites of all kinds including energy parasites.

Another mysterious quality attributed to it by certain crystal therapists is synchronicity as well as serendipity. It allows one to be at the right place at the right time. It also increases one's patience and teaches one the right timing to take action. It is very supportive during times of stress.

Usually, people who are exploring their inner selves and spirituality are attracted to it. This mysterious and mystical stone is a calming and protective companion for periods of transformation.

Lapis Lazuli: A Bolt from the Blue

To be able to speak the truth one has to be in touch with one's consciousness and higher- self first. This stunning blue rock, formed of various minerals (lazurite embedded in calcite and pyrites) does that wonderfully. The paradox of Lapis is that it clarifies conscious rational thought and at the same time awakens and enhances intuition. In every way it helps us see as it works on our third eye centre. It is also the stone par excellence for the throat centre where any blockage can affect communication. Lapis can aid the clearing and unblocking of this vocal centre in our bodies. The intense blue colour of Lapis comes from Lazurite which is formed when limestone comes into contact with calcite and pyrite. As Naisha Ahsian explains in *The Book of Stones*, calcite inclusions assist in clearing the energy system of the body to accommodate higher spiritual energies and pyrite inclusions assist in acting upon one's highest ideals and one's visions.

Lapis can sometimes be confused with Sodalite because Sodalite can be found as one of the minerals making Lapis. However, lapis has a brilliant blue hue in contrast to the dark depths of sodalite; also, Lapis has gold flecks because of the iron pyrites in it whereas Sodalite has white veins running within it. The name lapis comes from the Latin word for stone (lapis) and the Persian 'lazhuward"(meaning blue) which testifies to its multicultural roots. The name Lapis Lazuli became popular in the middle ages. The Greeks used to refer to the same stone as Sapphirus (sapphire). But lapis is a far older stone as it has been mined in Afghanistan (from where the finest Lapis comes even today) for nearly 6000 years and been used in Egypt in scarabs, beads , pendant and various burial ornaments of Kings and Queens as far back as 3100 B.C. It was also held in esteem by Sumerians, Assyrians and the Chinese. Used in powder form as medicine, cosmetic (eyeshadow) in Egypt, it was ground to form expensive paint, along with Azurite for Renaissance artists. Michel Angelo's works for example reveal Lapis as a component of the blue paint.

This, then, is the other paradox of Lapis as it resonates with the colour favoured by the creative artist, by ancient and European royalty as well the contemplative student or the solitary thinker. Some people like to carry it to auditions and anywhere one has to perform as an orator or singer as it is supposed to enhance skill as well as fame. Indigo and deep blues are associated with calm, tranquillity, inner vision, detachment and also especially in the case of Lapis the flash of intuition: the solution that strikes us like a bolt out of the blue literally.

Lapis can be worn to work not only because it looks cool and smart but because it attracts professional success and aids clear and effective communication. It helps one find one's voice and is especially helpful for empaths as it can clear the aura of any feelings picked from other people. It can bring about spiritual awakening and has been reported to aid dream recall as well as past life recall. It is a strong stone so if it is worn for long periods it could bring up issues that may leave some people feeling subdued but that is a part of one's evolution. On the other hand some people report it to be a great restorer of tranquillity and peace. Everyone should trust their own response to any crystal, whatever a book or a reader may tell them. Lapis is very effective for blocking psychic attack sending the negative energy back to the source. It can also help with relationships because of the role it plays in communication and clear thinking and also because it radiates harmony.

In healing it is a good stone for any healer to wear. It is credited with curing migraines and any vision related headaches. It is beneficial for the endocrine and nervous systems and especially for thyroid issues. Judy Hall also lists it as useful for alleviating depression and insomnia.

Brilliant blue Lapis lazuli is an ancient stone that still rocks. It helps us speak our truth with true understanding and compassion.

Moldavite: Out of This World

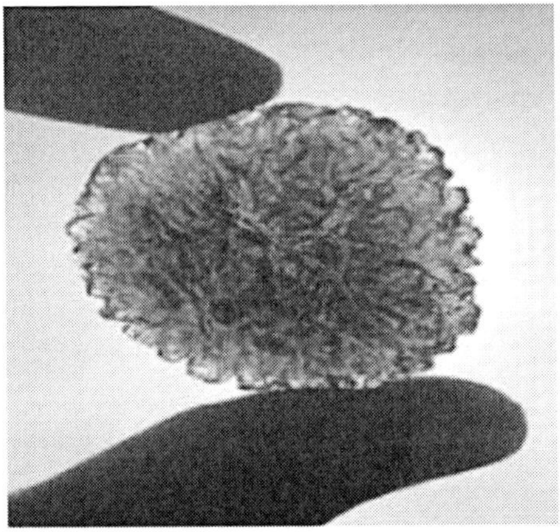

Moldavite cannot be explored without acknowledging the metaphysical aspects of crystals. This green glassy stone from the sky is one whose purpose is to make us aware of our connection to a world that lies outside our logical definition of the "real" world. It is also a very rare stone and is getting rarer because it is found only in the Czech Republic, near the Moldau river. It is a tektite (from the Greek tektos meaning molten) formed of silicon dioxide, aluminium oxide and some other metal oxides and impurities. Tektites are natural glasses thought to be formed from interplanetary collisions, and Moldavite is assumed to have originated from the crash of a large meteorite approximately 14.8 million years ago. This new age sounding stone was however, quite well known and prized in ancient and medieval cultures. Called "*agni mani*" in Sanskrit (though the term may have used loosely for all tektites), it was used across the world for tools, jewellery making and as protective amulets. Throughout the middle ages it was associated with the Holy Grail and only the nobility were allowed to wear it. Czech brides were gifted this stone as a betrothal gift for happy relationships.

Because of its rarity and the fact that it will soon become extinct, authentic pieces are very hard to find and expensive. Caution must be exercised when buying this stone especially online, as fakes abound. It has a rippled surface with craters. If the piece on sale is too large or shiny smooth it is likely a fake. Up to 3 grams is what one is most likely to find (and afford!). Pieces larger than 10 grams are rare and expensive. If the price sounds too good to be true it probably is.

Magic is a two edged sword and Moldavite energy is too magical and intense not to be felt. It is a swift acting stone and the term "Moldavite flush" describes some people's first reactions to the stone: a feeling of heat, headache, nausea, images flashing in the mind: though not all people feel that. A majority of the people soon get adjusted to its frequency and don't feel these symptoms; some never react in the first place. It affects everyone differently. Most users report vivid dreams and good dream recall, because it is the stone par excellence to connect us to metaphysical dimensions; and dreams, though more commonly linked to submerged aspects of ourselves in this "real" world, are also believed to connect us to our "other" self. People have used it to attempt astral projection and connecting to spirit. It enhances any meditation experience. Sometimes such connections can be dangerous. On the other hand, Moldavite takes us out of our comfort zone and brings to surface issues and roadblocks that need to be dealt with.

At a more immediate and practical level, Moldavite brings to light the cause of any disease and aids in releasing it. It brings to surface quickly and brutally whatever is blocking our progress at a spiritual level. Sometimes this may correspond with our idea of what is blocking us in the material world as well. For example, it may help remove people or situations who no longer serve us. Old friends may come back into our lives. We may be forced to abandon unhealthy behaviour or habits. Signs and synchronicities become more common. We may be led to meet people who we need to, professionally and personally, at that time. It might be a good idea to use the stone for brief intervals till one gets totally used to it.

A session with Moldavite is best completed by holding a grounding dark stone like Nuumiite, Haemetite, Black Tourmaline, a pair of Boji stones or Smoky Quartz because Moldavite can leave one dizzy and light headed if one is not attuned to its high vibration.

As pointed out before, take it or leave it, magical Moldavite can only be described in these extraordinary terms.

Moonstone

Known as *Chandrakanta* stone in Hindi, Moonstone has had a special place in Vedic astrology and was also known variously as a lover's stone, women's stone or the stone most associated with the moon. One myth suggests that this bluish hued white stone with its pretty play of light was formed from Bali's body when Rama killed Bali. Some of the best specimens still come from Sri Lanka.

Moonstone offers a quiet strength and resilience in times of stress especially when the cause is located in emotional turmoil. It helps recover hidden sources of strength within oneself. It helps people express the truth with tact and gentleness. Healers and sensitive helpful people are attracted to this stone and its feminine nurturing energies. It is very good for Inner-child work and healing childhood traumas. It is a stone that can help children sleep peacefully.

It offers slow and steady support to metabolism and is especially helpful in managing water retention, bloating, pms and is also helpful for mood swings. It can regulate menstrual cycles. Spiritually, it is great for enhancing intuition. Though women are more naturally attracted to it, it can be useful for men who want or need to work on emotions and emotional balance. In everyone it encourages gentle introspection and helps to see reasons for the patterns and cycles that we attract. It inspires patience and right timing. Everyone can benefit from connecting with their feminine self and nature is one of the messages of Moonstone. It stands by us in difficult times and lends loving support and intelligent intuition.

Obsidian: The Dark Mirror for Scrying the Self

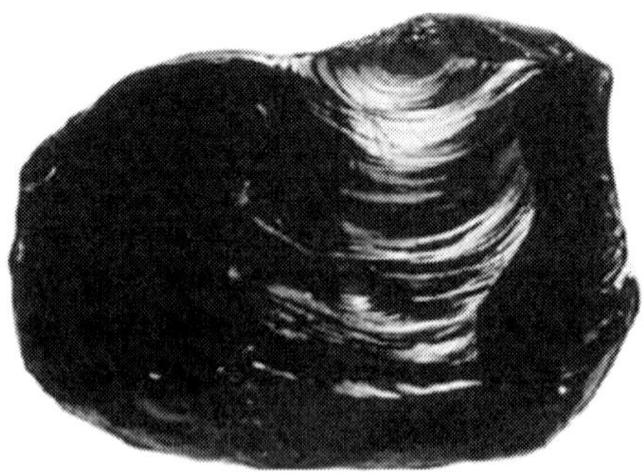

Obsidian is volcanic glass (and not technically a crystal) that has cooled so rapidly from molten lava, that it forms minimal crystals. Found within the margins of rhyolitic lava flows called obsidian flows, obsidian has long been used as a cutting and piercing tool, in ancient times, and even today in surgical scalpel tools. It has also been used in Shamanic ceremonies. It is believed to be good for scrying, that is sensing or seeing into a crystal, to access the cause of a problem in the past, or discerning knowledge about probable future outcomes. It is found not only in black colour but as mottled black and white (snowflake obsidian), brown (mahogany), iridescent rainbow obsidian, as well as in red-black, blue, blue-green, electric blue, gold sheen, green and apache tear varieties, all of which have additional healing properties, not included in this brief write-up.

Obsidian is not a stone for those afraid to see their shadow selves. It is supposed to be fast acting and brings hidden truths rushing to the surface, even unpleasant ones. It can reveal the cause of stress as well as disease but it persuades us to confront that cause, especially if it lies in behaviour patterns that do not serve us anymore. Clear quartz, used in conjunction with obsidian, can then help in resolution of those issues. For those who find black obsidian's effect too unsettling or sudden, a gentler form of obsidian like rainbow or mahogany or snowflake obsidian might be a better choice. It is the stone of transformation in every sense, and helps in seeing one's path in life, and in the process it sheds light on any patterns that might be blocking or draining us.

Obsidian is a grounding stone par excellence. Sue and Simon Lily point explain the grounding energy of red, brown and black stones by explaining their ability to direct and stabilize energy, thus:

> " Most healing work is concerned with the removal of inappropriate energy it tends to initiate deep levels of

> energy adjustment throughout many subtle systems of the body, bringing confusion, emotional instability and lack of focus. To avoid this discomfort healers take care to emphasize grounding and centring techniques to act as an anchor. Grounding ensures a firm contact with the energies of the planet so that excess energy can be conducted away from the body. It focuses on the present moment, practicality and connectedness to reality" (*Healing with Crystals*, pg 33).

The grounding ability of black crystals like Obsidian, Black Tourmaline and Haematite, can be enhanced by yoga postures that focus on balance in the lower body such as Tadaasana, and Vrikshasana, as well as on overall balancing as in Surya Namaskar.

Obsidian should not be worn for prolonged periods though because it may reduce activity in the wearer and induce inertia. Obsidian, like Black Tourmaline, is also an extremely protective stone. All forms of Obsidian protect from negativity of all kinds. When going through intense stress, or disease, holding obsidian can bring relief. It blocks psychic attack as well as protects one's body and possessions. It was worn as a talisman and as part of a shield by ancient priests. It helps healers because of its quick revelations and cathartic abilities.

In healing obsidian detoxifies, promotes digestion, removes blockages, including hardened arteries and relieves joint pain and the pain of arthritis. A protective, grounding stone that delves deep, it is best used for emotional release under supervision.

Rhodonite and Rhodochrocite : Healing the Heart

Rhodonite

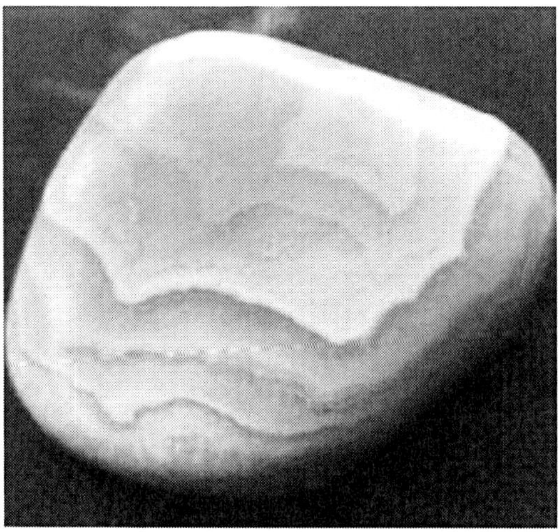

Rhodochrocite

"Strawberries, cherries and the angel's kiss in spring": go the lyrics of an old song. They could well describe the delicious pink hues of these two delectable crystals that help clear and balance the heart center.

Both Rhodonite {Mn^{+2},Fe^{+2},Mg,Ca)SiO_3} and Rhodochrocite ($MnCO_3$) are rich rose pink stones and both are manganese ores. Both seem to derive their name from the Greek word for "rose" (kros means colour).They can appear similar, but Rhodochrocite is more translucent, has white calcite inclusions and unlike Rhodonite, Rhodochrocite reacts to acids.

Rhodonite has pink mixed with red, brown and bands of black, in varying proportions. It works very well at the base and sacral chakras, is grounding and practical in its effect, but works mainly on the heart to balance a volatile emotional state. Sue and Simon Lily suggest that all pink stones including these two crystals and the softer, gentler rose quartz can help release stress by placing them wherever obvious tension is felt on the body. Take a deep breath in and visualize the breath coming in from the stone, absorbing the pink light. Feel the tensions melt and relax, every time you breathe out. Rose quartz can initiate a release and Rhodonite can stabilize it. One writer describes Rhodonite as the brick and mortar,that helps equilibrium every time our emotional states are shifting. It can remove self doubt, frustration of thwarted ambition, and resentment and anger arising from any cause. It is good for self-esteem and also diverts our attention away from the need to take revenge. Judy Hall terms it an excellent wound healer, and recommends it for joint problems, auto immune disease, stomach ulcers, multiple sclerosis and for healing or sensitizing hearing organs/auditory vibrations. I think Rhodonite is an excellent healer for past sexual trauma.

Rhodochrosite, also called manganese spar, appears similar to Rhodonite, but whereas the former has black or brown veins, Rhodochrosite has a predominance of cream or white banded zones, as well as orange, peach and red zones in differing striations. It has calcium, iron and magnesium added to its manganese content. Its colouring helps it blend the energies of base, sacral and solar plexus chakras, especially when emotional stress is causing havoc. According to Sue and Simon Lily, it helps anxious individuals, whose tensions affect digestive and reproductive areas of the body. It also works to soothe any fears about one's safety and increases self-confidence. It increases self knowledge, identifying the patterns and purpose behind certain ongoing experiences in life. It encourages one to bring to the surface all that has been repressed, including irrational fears and emotions that one does not want to accept. It is also supposed to attract a soul mate to one self, but a soul mate experience is not always a bed of roses. It is love that teaches us, and works for our highest growth and good. Overall, it is a happy stone, lifting depression. Judy Hall, has listed the physical ailments that Rhodochrocite works on: respiratory problems, migraines (because it dilates blood vessels) and blood pressure. For migraines it needs to be kept on top of the spine. It purifies the circulatory system and kidneys and restores poor eyesight.

Both these crystals are heart healing, tension relieving and help with issues of co-dependency and abuse. Like Rose Quartz, they are also soothing to have around in the room, especially in the form of spheres.

Rose Quartz and Other Stones: Crystals for Love

Can crystals help us attract and keep love? Is there one magic stone that can help bring excitement to a boring life or nurturing and healing love to a broken heart? The answer is NO, and any such claims are generally a rip off. However, if one is willing to seek guidance and work on changing one's own perceptions and patterns, crystals can help attract and sustain loving relationships with oneself, one's family, friends, partner or spouse. They do so

by helping change our vibes and by aiding emotional healing. When one is happy, centred, open and willing to accept and offer unconditional love the results can be quite magical indeed. On the other hand, insecurities, long held guilt, sadness, anger or resentment are a ticking bomb for physical as well as emotional ailments.

As is well known, Rose Quartz is the crystal that tops the list in terms of popularity and effectiveness when it comes to being a "love stone". Associated with the Greek goddess Aphrodite, its reputation is well earned as it promotes peace and emotional well being, used for post natal depression as well as mid life crisis. It works by promoting self love and forgiveness of the self. Radiating unconditional love it attracts it in turn. Wearing it on the heart is supposed to be especially effective. However, one must always trust one's intuition and use a stone only if it feels comfortable. Though it is a gentle crystal, it can never the less bring emotions rushing to the surface if they have been held in too long. Secondly, wearing or holding the crystal can bring clarity to issues in a relationship, but the follow up work has to be done by a person, once the stone has enhanced our empathic ability to see things. Sometimes it may reveal the red flags in a relationship and help us face the truth.

Feng -Shui practitioners recommend placing a Rose Quartz crystal in the relationship corner which is farthest right corner from the entrance of a house or a room. Judy Hall claims that Rose Quartz can attract so much loving attention that it may need an amethyst to calm things down so that only the more appropriate energies come into one's orbit. One's own experience with crystals is the best guide as it may vary from that of others.

In healing Rose quartz wands radiate a gentle but firm healing energy that works in subtle ways. It is strengthening for the physical heart and is a good post-operative stone to keep in one's recovery room in the form of a sphere or tumbled stones. It is calming, de-tressing and quite good to assist with regulating blood pressure.

Pink tourmaline is another crystal that heals abuse and promotes love especially sensual love. So does Watermelon Tourmaline which with its pink and green colours balances the physical and emotional aspects of love. For sheer passion and enhancing sensuality, Ruby and Carnelian might be better choices. Rhodochrosite helps increase self –worth. Aventurine is also heart protecting and heart healing and also brings in sheer luck in all matters including romance. Malachite can help release painful memories and past hurt. If emotions have been held in too long ,Rhodocrocite can teach us to breathe comfortably again. Unakite and Malachite along with quartzes can help release emotional debris.

Sugilite, like Rose quartz and Rhodochrosite, is used to attract a soul mate, but soul mate relationships are not everlasting love stories. They are more like karmic connections that help us grow in this life, and may in fact often be intense and brief relationships, with lessons to teach us, as all relationships do. Kunzite (pink) and Larimar (blue, green or grey) both possess an ethereal beauty, and help heal hurts from past lives that may be impacting present relationships. Kunzite clears emotional residue and is mood lifting and protective of sensitive people (note: it is much more expensive than Rose Quartz). Chrysocolla is a great at balancing the heart chakra and healing past hurt and Peridot helps resolve jealousy and anger.

All these crystals work primarily on the heart chakra, the seat of our emotions. When we are healed and whole, we can't help but attract love and learn to both receive and give it.

Ruby

Regal ruby has always had pride of place in precious gemstone collections all over the world, including most notably in ancient and medieval Indian kingdoms. Vedic astrology places a high premium on a clear, well cut and polished ruby, making it more expensive than diamonds. It is a stone associated with the sun in Indian astrology and Ayurveda. However, semiprecious and raw ruby is more affordable and from the perspective of crystal therapy, just as effective: though not all are likely to agree with this observation. Technically, ruby is a corundum i.e. an aluminium oxide silicate that is constituted of chromium, iron and titanium. The pink, plum and reddish brown corundums are called rubies (various shades arising from titanium giving the pink and iron giving the dark red colouring in varying proportions) and all other coloured corundums are called sapphires.

Ruby is the stone par excellence for imparting motivation, vitality and a zest for life. It gives strength to the heart in both the physical sense and the emotional sense. Its red colour makes it a good base chakra (survival and indomitable courage) stone and also a blood detoxifier. It also works powerfully on the heart chakra. Its protection is therefore bestowed on both fronts: it protects during legal conflict and physical attack (Mars) and it protects from psychic attack as well as emotional draining of the heart (especially by people who are psychic vampires).In professional life it aids in increasing self -esteem and clarity.

Ruby is also associated with enhancing passion and sensuality. It increases potency, vigour and physical stamina in people who tire easily. Paradoxically, it can calm hyper people, aid concentration in restless people and add a practical perspective to a creative enterprise.

In healing it works on blood, lymph, fevers, the nervous and circulatory systems, infections and blisters. It stimulates the adrenals and kidneys. It is of special use to peri-menopausal and menopausal women and as Cassandra Eason puts it, "in helping older women value their beauty and life experiences". It banishes nightmares and assists lucid dreaming.

Children and animals are believed to be too sensitive to Ruby as it has been said to overstimulate. It may increase anger and possessiveness in some folks. As always, common sense, alertness and intuition must be exercised while using any precious stone or crystal as they can affect some people powerfully.

By helping recovery from past hurt and boosting confidence and motivation, this majestic stone empowers the heart in more ways than one.

Ruby in Zoisite

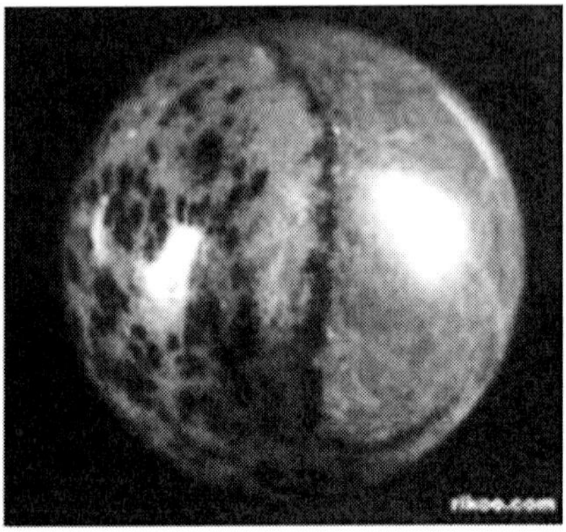

Ruby in Zoisite or Anyolite is a happy combination in the crystal kingdom. Easily available as it is sourced from India (as well as Tanzania. Australia and South Africa) and also easily affordable in tumble stone form, it is an attractive coming together of green zoisite (chromium and vanadium) and pinkish, reddish or violet hued ruby (corundum) with small black flecks. It weds the passion and life giving energies of ruby with the patience, growth, fertility and healing associated withZoisite. Primarily, green Zoisite is a heart chakra stone and Ruby a base chakra one but both are also associated with enhancing the psychic potential linked to the third eye and crown chakras and sexual and emotional balance linked to the sacral chakra. The word zois comes from the name of the mineral collector FreiherrZois who found this stone in Austria at the end of the eighteenth century.

All crystals may not emanate the same energy and properties for all users, and sometimes the same crystal may vary in its impact according to size or different proportions of mineral composition. Hence, these columns on crystals do not claim to be universally applicable but only bring together different crystal lovers' (including mine) responses to individual crystals. I find the energy of this stone very re-assuring, palpable and soothing after periods of emotional stress. Most have reported this as a joyous life affirming stone. It is perceived as a manifestation stone because it brings the heart's desire (zoisite) in touch with the go getting energies of the mind (ruby), thus helping us find ways to achieve our goals. Cassandra Eason says that " it gives us the strength of mind to pursue our dreams while keeping us still connected to the real world and balancing our own needs to fulfil our unique blue print with those of others around us"(*The New Crystal Bible*,315). To the general description of this stone as being good for reproductive disorders especially libido and infertility in both men and women (for which it can be worn or kept at the bedside), Eason adds a few more points. It brings healing after abortion or miscarriage, also after hysterectomy or early menopause. It is good overall for "sexual dilemmas; helps young people to accept if they want to resolve worries about trans- or bisexuality" (Eason,315) or about sexuality in general.

Ruby invigorates the body and mind giving vitality. Zoisite , according to Michael Gienger, helps us to "avoid conforming to others", to be "creative" wherever we have left off doing so, "it transforms destructive attitudes into constructive ones" and "hinders inflammation and strengthens the immune system" but it "takes a while to unfold its full effects so only continued use will ensure success" (*Crystal Power*,400). I personally find Ruby in Zoisite to be instantly uplifting.

Robert Simmons sees it as a stone that harmonizes and stimulates the root, heart and third eye chakras thereby enhancing intuitive abilities, the "intensity of the heart's yearning", empathy and compassion, energizing the body and also of becoming aware of and releasing grief. Simmons recommends it for assisting with the treatment of depression, exhausted adrenals, chronic fatigue, sluggish thyroid and fainting spells (*The Book of Stones*, 436-437).

Rosy green Ruby in Zoisite increases the potency of one's energy field and helps us relate to others while keeping our boundaries intact. It protects us while travelling and at the workplace by making us pause before we act(Zoisite probably checking any indiscretion or risk taking propelled by Ruby perhaps)and then we act with full conviction. This stone brings together minerals that join in a sacred marriage of partners that complement each other and infuse life and healing.

Selenite

Serene Selenite is an excellent protective stone to have by one's bedside. It is named after the ancient Greek Moon Goddess Selene. A hydrous calcium sulphate mineral, it is a form of gypsum and is closely related to fibrous gypsum, also called Satin Spar. When clear and well- formed it is called Selenite and its very fine grained large form it is called Alabaster. Selenite can be colourless, white, peach (peach and white are commonly sold in India), grey, green or blue (blue is quite rare). It is a very fragile crystal that dissolves and disintegrates in water so washing it should be avoided. Simply running incense smoke around it should clear it effectively.

It is a crystal that resonates with the higher chakras and opens one's intuition, connection to the Universe and also works on the Soul Star chakra. It is a stone par excellence to connect to one's guides and receive higher guidance. It even looks like a pillar of prayer, a link between the self and God. Healers can use it like a healing wand to clear blockages in the etheric body and also to scan the aura. It is a great stone to meditate with. It both inspires and protects. In everyday life it gets energy moving and helps us move forward in life with conviction and divine guidance. It can calm and at the same time prevent stagnation and blockages. It is healing for the nervous system and the brain. It can jumpstart meditation and help one progress in it. In case one feels lightheaded on using it, a grounding stone like smoky quartz or black tourmaline can be held in the hand. Just keeping it in the room can increase positive vibrations in one's aura and living space.

It is believed to be helpful for hormone regulation in women and aids with pregnancy, helps relieve pms and regulate menstrual cycles.

It protects from negativity and disturbing dreams and helps bring restful slumber to adults and children alike. Sleep with Selenite or meditate with it to awake the higher self.

Seraphinite

Seraphinite is a prominent overall healing stone in new age lore. Seraphims are the highest orders of the angels and the stone Seraphinite derives its name from angels' wings because this green stone is actually feathery to touch. It has silvery white feather like lines running through its green hued surface. Its older pagan name is Clinochlore from the Greek words klino (oblique lines) and chloros (green). Seraphinite is primarily a silicate but a complex one: Magnesium Aluminium Iron Silicate Hydrooxide with white feathery inclusions of mica.

Its fern green colour makes it a premium heart chakra stone but its healing and uplifting powers are not confined to a single organ or energy centre. In fact it is supposed to heal at an auric level and is especially useful for the crown and soul star chakras. On an emotional level, it is a good ally to have during rough periods in relationships. It has a gentle, soothing, angelic presence and it helps dispel negativity. It helps us find our way out of the emotional stress caused by other people and work our way out of feelings of abandonment, guilt and accusations. It is believed to help us refine our relationship with angelic forces of the Universe as well as with nature spirits. It is an excellent dream recall stone.

On a physical level it is supposed to aid regeneration at a cellular level. It helps in longstanding health conditions and some crystal workers attribute this to its ability to reveal the source of disease in past lives and to initiate healing. It works on the spine and its connection with the auric body. It helps release tension in the upper back and shoulders. Judy Hall says that it also helps promote weight loss.

A gentle healing stone that promotes harmony and friendship, it is a good aid for meditation especially nature meditation. Its healing works by encouraging soul enlightenment and self awareness. Meditating while looking into its feathery depths should bring many benefits: there is more to Seraphinite than meets the eye.

Serpentine

Revered as a protective stone in many ancient cultures and used widely in the form of amulets, jewellery and seals (in Mesopotamia, Egypt and Greece for example), Serpentine is believed to have the magical property of drawing out toxins and protecting from snake bite. A Greek poem written in 4th C AD, attributed to the mythical Orpheus celebrates "powdered serpentine" for curing any wound inflicted by "the reptile race". This belief probably underlies this stone's unusual and possibly scary name. But then, it also looks like serpent skin as it is usually found in mottled green and brown shades, with an oily or waxy texture. Serpentine or Magnesium iron silicate hydroxide can be found in shades of red, yellow, white, black mixed in a hue of greens. Vessels made from Serpentine were used in Roman time because it was believed that they cracked when they came in contact with poisons. Pottery made from black Serpentine is still used in Manipur and is usually available at places like Dilli Haat. Even today Serpentine is credited with the ability to drive out toxins, and to eliminate hair and gut parasites and protect from poisons.

In meditation Serpentine is supposed to alleviate the discomfort arising from the Kundalini rising too quickly. However, such practices must be closely supervised as the Kundalini is not something to be played around with. Keeping Serpentine near one's feet is supposed to improve one's connection with the earth and keeping it near the crown and third eye is supposed to enhance meditation and trance experiences. Some believe it helps with past life recall and helps access between-lives healing.

Emotionally, like all green stones it aids relationships and helps correct emotional imbalances. An interesting aspect is this stone's effect in enhancing self confidence, taking the right decision in a situation of conflict and protection from people who drain one's energy as well as from fraudsters: an extension of its ability to eliminate parasites and parsiticism. It also helps with bingeing and obesity which has an emotional basis. It helps in new beginnings as symbolically a snake shedding its skin moves effortlessly ahead.

It is a healing stone which helps in magnesium and calcium absorption. Cassandra Eason also mentions its uses in Alzeimer's and senile dementia. It also aids in regulating sugar metabolism. It is cleansing and detoxifying at all levels.

Serpentine brings us closer to nature. Mysterious and healing serpentine can bring joy if you connect with this scaly veined marvel.

Smoky Quartz: Grounding The Self

Solid support for stressful times is at hand with Smoky Quartz. All quartz is healing and together with amethyst, rose quartz and clear quartz, smoky quartz is a valuable part of any collection. While clear quartz radiates and amplifies energy,

smoky quartz is an expert at attracting pain, negativity and blockages away from the body into itself. It needs to be cleansed when used thus as it works quietly but very quickly at calming worries and lifting stress.Easily available, smoky quartz is a silicon dioxide (Si O_2) mineral, and is naturally radiated (quartz) of a colour varying from translucent brown, to blackish hued dark brown or yellowing hued translucent stone. The darker varieties might be artificially radiated.

Smoky quartz is above all a grounding stone par excellence. Here, it may be useful to quote Naisha Ahsian :

> "Like the smoke of a sage bundle, the energy of smoky quartz cleanses and clears the aura and energetic systems. It assists one in connecting to the earth and completing the electrical circuit between pone's physical body and the planet. Without this completed circuit, one's energy systems are very much like a high tension power line that has been snapped. Though there is plenty of energy available, there is nowhere for it to go. By grounding one completes the circuit, gives the excess energy a safe outlet and re-establishes a healthy energetic flow in the body" (*The Book of Stones*, Simmons &Ahsian, California:North Atlantic Books, 1998).

Grounding is necessary for anyone who is a healer and also anyone who over uses the higher chakras of the logical and creative mind as well as psychic intuition. Ruby, Garnet, Black Tourmaline, Obsidian, Smoky Quartz are some of the many options available in the crystal world for this purpose and the stone must be chosen by intuiting. One size does not fit all in the crystal kingdom. Certain yogic postures involving balancing on one's legs, tai chi, squats, lunges and Pilates are also grounding, as is visualizing tree roots or being near them.

Meditating with or placing Smoky Quartz near oneself should make one feel more centred, aware, balanced and calm. Smoky Quartz is not possibly a good choice for increasing energy for athletic pursuits or increasing dynamism for outer activities. And yet, it helps fitness enthusiasts as a pain reliever for muscle cramps. It balances out the tendency to be too much in the head by drawing awareness within. It enhances discretion and judgement in physical and mental activities.

It is a highly protective stone for sensitive people and healers. It helps one maintain healthy boundaries and separate one's own issues from another person's. It puts things in perspective overall.

Smoky Quartz is believed to be healing for the lower body especially for the abdomen, fungal infections, hips, legs, back pain, diseases of the kidneys and pancreas, piles and sexual trauma. It helps in the assimilation of minerals and fluid regulation. It is supposed to fortify the muscles and nerves. A lot of therapists claim that it is useful in counteracting the effects of radiotherapy (as in chemotherapy) and also of electromagnetic radiation at home. One's own experience should guide the use of crystals as has been pointed out in these columns before.

When the going gets tough, smoky quartz can lift pessimism and negativity and help one believe that the tough phase will pass. It is an excellent aid for stress and. building resilience. It helps us slow down, take stock of the situation and helps rid one's aura of negativity and allows us to move ahead with a sense of calm power.

Sugilite

Sugilite is a crystal of extraordinary colouring, usually purple to violet pink in colour, though darker hues are also found. It gets this eye-catching beauty from the complex mix of minerals that form it: potassium, sodium, manganese, iron, aluminium lithium silicate, expressed as the chemical formula $KNa_2(Fe^{2+},Mn^{2+},Al)_2Li_3Si_{12}O_{30}$. Most commonly found in manganese mines in South Africa, the manganese content makes it a good healing stone for headaches.

That is just the tip of the iceberg, however. Magical healing properties are ascribed to this stone, which has been linked to the "violet ray of transmutation and transformation", according to Simone Matthews and many others who have meditated with it. It is most useful for those who find the world a strange and hostile place, which makes it useful for paranoia and schizophrenia, unlike amethyst, another violet purple stone which should not be used, as it increases sensitivity. Sugilite helps deal with sensitivity at all levels, which makes it an excellent protective stone for empaths. It helps balance mainly the pituitary, but also adrenal and pineal glands and the right and left hemispheres of the brain. It assists in the healing of autism and dyslexia. A person with Asperger's syndrome might find it easier to communicate with Sugilite. It reduces hostility and anger in oneself and offers strong protection from these emotions coming from others as well as negative entities. People who find it difficult to deal with technology or environment related pollution, a discomfort that usually manifests as allergy or general discomfort, can find an ally in Sugilite. For example, one can use it with turquoise for someone who gets a sty (eyes) from being near computers and air conditioners.

If you feel a sense of disinterest in what you are working on or doubt, Sugilite may just spark the joy and drive to finish your project. Although, it is usually described in metaphysical, not practical terms, as a crystal for discovering one's divine purpose in this life, and for aligning oneself with universal love, hence its other name lovulite. Some combinations that have been used:

With Amethyst for extra psychic protection, and also to overcome addictions used with Amethyst, Tourmaline or Unakite; Even by itself it is believed to help with addictions to shopping, alcohol and gambling.

With Seraphinite for healing;

With Shattuckite for channelling;

With Hematite for grounding;

It must be noted that the user's needs must be taken into account. For example if ones higher chakras are too vibrant, then grounding becomes very important to balance the upper chakras with the base chakras. If instead one wants to go into trance meditation, Moldavite can be used with Sugilite (the deep purple kind). One's own comfort with the crystal and gut feeling is very important. And also what intent is set in programming a crystal for oneself.

Sugilite is said to alleviate despair in cancer patients. To anyone who is not at ease with this world, sugilite helps integration with others. It also helps discover and break old patterns that cause disease and hold us back from achieving our potential. It encourages loving sentiments and a patient compassion. It helps forgive: and forgiveness is divine.

Sunstone

Sunstone is a crystal connected with sunlight and has a sparkling yellow - orange colour. Usually the crystal is lighter at both ends and darker orange brown in the middle with almost red reflections in between. It must be distinguished from what is commonly called sunstone in Indian markets: that shiny yellow and dark - brown stone. It is the crystal of joy, bringing hope to the mind and vitality to the body. It increases the body's self - healing powers and is particularly useful for stomach ulcers and chronic colds. It helps in alleviating cartilage related as well as general aches and pain.

Sunstone is linked specifically to the solar plexus and sacral chakras. Using Sunstone to unblock these chakras can relieve the problems associated with a blockage in this area, such as excess weight around the middle, digestive problems, stomach ulcers and hormonal imbalances. It also brings the solar chakra in harmony with the sacral chakra (four fingers below the navel), thus balancing emotions and instinct with thoughts and a sense of self. It increases confidence and makes the wearer more attractive. According to Ahsian, it makes one place service before self and teaches how to use one's talents and energies to help others.

Sunstone is especially useful for removing energy hooks or preventing energy drawing by possessive friends, partners or family members. It fosters independence in the wearer and those around them and can contribute to forming relationships that are for one's higher good, rather than those that are detrimental to one's personality.

Some people like to keep their sunstone with a moonstone, thus bringing together their respective yang and yin properties: power, hope, passion balanced by love, peace and spirituality. One should use one's gut feeling or first instinct when picking up or combining crystals.

Sunstone is supposed to work best in the sunlight, bringing its energy to permeate all aspects of one's life. It is a crystal that removes self-doubt and encourages healing, optimism, warmth, happiness and the constructive use of one's strength and creativity. Like Carnelian it is a crystal of exuberance, creativity and fun.

Turquoise

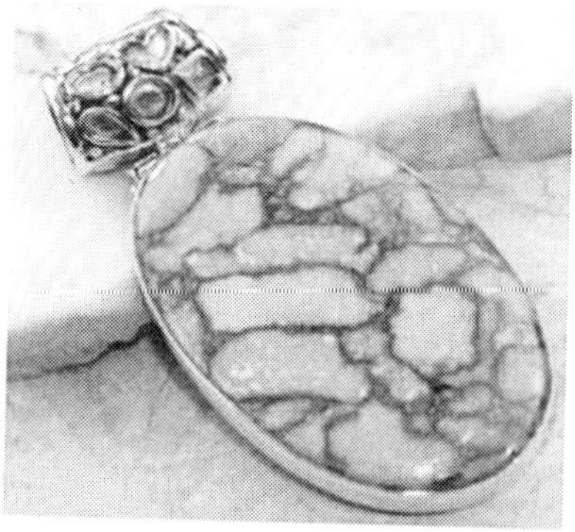

Chances are that most readers are already familiar with this popular stone, which is widely used in jewellery and is called *Firoza* in Hindi. One of the first gemstones to be mined, its history as a spiritual stone can be traced back to over 7500 years ago. It was highly revered by the Native Americans, Tibetans and Egyptians among other cultures. Turquoise is a copper aluminium phosphate mineral. It is a very pretty and soothing blue stone, ranging between blue and green depending on whether copper (blue, Persian usually) or iron (more green, Tibetan usually) predominates.

Turquoise has always been valued as an all-round protective stone, especially for its associations with travelling and horse riding (Native American belief). It is believed to cleanse and align the energy centres/chakras, with the unusual ability to ground even as the energy path is kept open. So while it is tranquil and calming, it is also a vibrant and happy stone. Though as pointed before, crystals reveal their properties to their user, and this is especially true of Turquoise, which promotes the ability to be still and listen to oneself. Being a blue stone, it works on the throat chakra and aids truth telling as well as creative expression and communication. It is supposed to draw out illness and negative energy wherever it is placed on the body, and works on detoxifying from alcohol, poison and pollutants. It has been used as a good luck charm and a protective stone since centuries.

At an emotional level, it brings positivity, helping deal with mood swings. It prevents an attitude of self-sabotage and martyrdom, encouraging self-knowledge and self-control.

Some of its healing benefits:

- Heals headaches
- Cataracts and eye problems
- Alleviates stomach problems, cramps and pains
- Immunity builder overall
- Sore throats cleared and soothed
- Tissue regeneration
- Aids nutrient absorption
- Gout, rheumatism healed because it works on hyperacidity & is anti-inflammatory

Turquoise helps with seeing (3rd eye chakra), expression (throat), feeling clear and positive (heart), and with protection from toxins (solar). Turquoise helps us accept all aspects of ourselves and brings the gift of vitality. It helps us articulate well and socializes with others. At the same time it is a stone of spiritual awareness and opens one to the infinite blue of the sky thus inducing a feeling of oneness with the Universe.

A Special Note

I would like to thank Meetu Sehgal, my Reiki teacher and friend for guiding me and also for giving permission to rework and use some of the material I had already published in her e-magazine *Kaleidoscope*. I would also like to thank Yulia (Ioulia) Pal, my Prana Therapy teacher, for enhancing my knowledge of using crystals for healing. I thank my husband Ajay and son Agastya for their continued support and love.

Bibliography

"Ancient India's Contribution to Astronomy", http://mathemajik.googlepages.com/astronomy.htm. 2, Bhrigusamhita

Bruce Scofield. "Were They Astrologers? — Big League Scientists and Astrology", *The Mountain Astrologer magazine.* http://www.mountainastrologer.com/standards/editor's%20choice/articles/science_ast.html

David Pingree, "The Dictionary of the History of Ideas, Astrology", https://hi.wikipedia.org/https://in.pinterest.com/narendragaekwad/nakshtras/

Eason, Cassandra, *The New Crystal Bible: 500 Crystals to Heal Your Body, Mind and Spirit*, London: Carlton Books, 2010.

Grienger, Michael, *Crystal Power Crystal Healing: The Complete Handbook*, London: Cassell, 1998.

Hall, Judy, *The Crystal Bible: The Definitive Guide to Crystals*, London: Godsfield, 2003.

Lilly, Sue and Simon, *Healing with Crystal and Chakra Energies*, London: Hermes House, 2010.

Livingston, John W. (1971), "Ibn Qayyim al-Jawziyyah: A Fourteenth Century Defense against Astrological Divination and Alchemical Transmutation", *Journal of the American Oriental Society*, 91 (1): 96–103, doi:10.2307/600445

Michael Star, "Astrology FAQ, Basics for Beginners and Students of Astrology".

Pandit Kewal Krishan, *Nakshtra Vigyan*, New Delhi, 1991.

Reinhold Ebertin (1994), *Combination of Stellar Influences*. Tempe, Ariz.: American Federation of 12 Astrologers.

Robert Hand, "The History of Astrology — Another View", http:/ www.zodiacal.com/articles/hand/history.htm.

S.C. Mishra, *Jatak Parijat*, Vol 1 & 2.

Saliba, George, *A History of Arabic Astronomy: Planetary Theories During the Golden Age of Islam*, New York University Press, 1997.

Simmons, Robert & Naisha Ahsian, *The Book of Stones: Who They Are & What They Teach*, Berkeley: North Atlantic Books, 2005, 2007.

Surkant Jha, *Nakshtra Vigyan*, New Delhi.

आईसेंक, एच. जे., नियास, डी.के.बी, *ज्योतिष : विज्ञान या अंधविश्वास?*, पेंगुइन बुक्स, 1982

एसपाइन्स (सितंबर 1964), *अलबिरूनी के अनुसार खगोल विज्ञान और ज्योतिष के बीच अन्तर शब्दार्थिक अन्तर*, आइसिस 55 (3) : 343-349

डेविडपिन्ग्री, एस्ट्रलओ मेंस से ज्योतिष तक, बेबीलोन से बीकानेर तक, रोमा : इस्तितुतोइतलि अनोपरल 'अफ्रीकाऐल' ओरिएंटे, 1997

वी. के. चौधरी, के. राजेश चौधरी, 2006, जन्मपत्री बताने वाली प्रणाली दृष्टिकोण, सिस्टम एप्रोच (आस्ट्रोलोजी) सिस्टम्स एप्रोच फॉर इन्तेर्प्रेटिंग होरोस्कोप्स *(Systems' Approach (astrology)Systems' Approach for Interpreting Horoscopes)* चौथा संशोषित अंक, सागर प्रकाशन, नई दिल्ली, भारत।

Websites

rainbowcrystal.com
charmsoflighthealing.com
en.wikipedia.org